THE **FACTS** OF **LIVE**

HOW LIVE EVENTS ARE CONCEIVED, PROCURED AND PRODUCED TO CREATE THE GREATEST VALUE AND IMPACT

WILL GLENDINNING

RETHINKPRESS

First published in Great Britain 2018
by Rethink Press (www.rethinkpress.com)

Cover concept: Dejan Jovanovic
Cover artwork: Will Glendinning

Illustrations and diagrams: Will Glendinning

Portrait photo: Sean Ebsworth Barnes

Contents

Disclaimers

The book (*The Facts Of Live*), the website www.TheFactsOfLive.com and any related or associated materials (Work) contain the opinions and ideas of Will Glendinning (Author) as published by Rethink Press (Publisher). The Work is intended as a reference guide providing helpful and informative material. The information and strategies outlined in the Work may not be suitable for every individual, organisation, business or situation, and are not guaranteed or warranted to produce any particular results. Neither the Author nor the Publisher is providing or offering legal, financial, accounting, safety, security or other professional advice or services through the Work. You should consult a competent professional before adopting any of the suggestions in the Work or drawing inferences from them.

No warranty is made with respect to the accuracy or completeness of the information or references contained within the Work, and, to the extent permitted by law, all statutory warranties are expressly excluded (including those relating to fitness for a particular purpose). References to any external organisation or website as a citation or source of further information do not mean that the Author or Publisher endorses the information these external sources provide. External websites, in particular, may have changed between the time the Work was published and the time they are accessed by the reader. Both the Author and the Publisher specifically disclaim any responsibility for any liability, loss or damage, whether personal, professional or otherwise, incurred as a consequence, directly or indirectly, of the use or application of the Work or the advice contained within the Work.

Praise For Will Glendinning and The Facts Of Live

'As one of the industry's thought leaders, Will Glendinning has the ability to make complex situations, problems and live events simple in an instant. His leadership talents are some of the best I have come across and he's one of the few people I trust implicitly. If you're involved with live events or thinking about it, this book is essential reading.'

Olivier Vallée
Former Vice President and Managing Director
George P Johnson

'Will's expertise creating and delivering major events which are becoming increasingly complex and risky, has been proven time and time again. As well as bringing clarity to often challenging situations, he also genuinely cares about everyone, which reassures and empowers an event's stakeholders and supports the growth of the in-house capabilities of the organisations involved.'

Zara Hyde Peters OBE
Former CEO British Triathlon
Non-Executive Director, Birmingham Organising Committee –
2022 Commonwealth Games

'Will has a personable and sensitive approach that makes his guidance regarding all aspects of live events, from the creative and practical to the commercial and political, insightful, hugely valuable and – importantly – accessible. From complex major events to subtler, more delicate, cultural events, Will always provides innovative solutions and ideas, and cuts through the noise, focusing everyone on exactly what matters with clarity, helping all involved improve their game and in turn the quality and impact of any event.'

Amanda Lumley
Director, Tourism Management Institute

'The power of cultural events to reimagine places, strengthen communities and transform lives is well known. Working with Will Glendinning on the delivery of the London 2012 cultural festival – the biggest and most accessible outdoor festival ever delivered in London – he brought leadership and expertise to enable the delivery of 2,500 events in places and spaces across the landscape of Greater London. His personable, flexible and knowledgeable approach helped steer projects of all scales through a challenging and often complex political environment, and had the result of protecting the integrity of artists' work and creative direction, as well as strengthening long-term understanding and legacy partnerships for future programmes. His approach allows leaders of major events to push boundaries and innovate, and offers the support, guidance and safety net necessary to do so – regardless of the scale of the challenge or ambition.'

Chenine Bhathena
Creative Director, Coventry City of Culture 2021
Former Senior Cultural Strategy Officer, Greater London Authority

'In The Facts Of Live, Will Glendinning unpicks exactly what it takes to create the most powerful live events possible. If you're involved with live events or exhibitions in any way this book might just inspire you to rethink how you approach things. Even with the relentless and accelerating advancement of digital channels, live events are an increasingly important and popular component of our culture, as brands look to create engaging real-world connections and experiences. Will's creativity, coupled with his energy and enthusiasm to push the boundaries of live events in all their forms, never wavers, and whether you're client or agency-side, this book demonstrates how, where and when you're best focusing your own energy and efforts.'

Adrian Bell
Co-Founder and Executive Director, Action Impact

'I have known and worked with Will for many years. Having myself led some of the biggest events on Earth from the sharp end, if there's one thing I know for sure: it's a field many people think or proclaim they're an expert in. In Will Glendinning though the term 'expert' is not only justified, but proven, time and time again, and in all manner of situations and scenarios. He constantly strives to innovate and elevate the work of everyone around him. Creative and insightful, Will works and imparts his expertise without turning it into a dark art and always with surgical precision; exactly where and when it's needed; all with a level of humility that belies the true power that comes with the breadth of his experience and talents.'

Kris Donaldson
Director, Partnership Development – INSEAD
Former Chief Executive Officer, Liverpool European Capital of Culture 2008
Former General Manager, Marketing and Sponsorship, Sydney 2000 Olympic Games

'Will effortlessly and seamlessly dovetails the temporary and transient world of live events with the permanent world of construction, calling upon his diverse experience within both. His ability to direct and balance commercial, practical and creative thinking is incredibly valuable when it comes to placemaking and the feasibility and design of public realm and commercial property developments.'

Anna Strongman
Partner, Argent LLP Property Developers

'Will is unflappable and a brilliant problem solver. In an industry rife with last-minute changes, his exceptional emotional intelligence and empathy with what everyone involved with a live event goes through helps him focus people on what matters, steering them through the lot, making it look easy when it most definitely is not.'

Natalie Melton
Former Commercial Director, Arts & Business
Co-Founder and Deputy Chairman, The New Craftsmen

'Will has taken the subject of live events – a subject, industry and craft so broad, complex and unwieldy – and, remarkably, managed to tame and codify it in the most authentic, direct and simple way. Based on facts and Will's experience, *The Facts Of Live* is mandatory reading: an elegant, insightful and actionable go-to reference guide for anyone looking to procure live events or improve how theirs are produced.'

Dr Efrosyni Konstantinou
Senior Lecturer in Strategic Management of Projects
University College London

Glossary

There is very little terminology universally adopted or understood when discussing live events, and it would be easy to pick holes in the details contained in *The Facts Of Live* if one were to focus on certain titles, words and terms. For this reason, I must point out that it's the spirit of what I discuss in the pages of this book that's important rather than specific terms, titles or definitions.

This is a book, though, and books need words. For clarity, I have listed a few of the words used throughout *The Facts Of Live* below, along with their definitions in the context of the book's content.

Agency: An individual or company appointed to produce all or part of a live event. An agency's duties may include creating ideas, strategies and concepts, development and planning, delivery and management.

Client: The person or organisation paying for or underwriting an event. For example, a brand would be the client for its marketing event, an artist would be the client (assuming they are paying) for their arts or entertainment event, and an organising committee would be the client if they are paying for elements of an event they are organising (producing) themselves.

Commission: To outsource a live event. Commissioning is the act of paying for an event to be produced. Commissioning may be a brand hiring an event agency, an individual paying for someone to create a new sporting event, or a government paying for the development and delivery of a summit.

Content: The purpose of an event, for example the message at a conference, the music at a concert, or the art at an art exhibition.

Context:

The backdrop or environment in which an event is to be staged, be that physical, financial, operational or political. Put simply, the content is the event's purpose, the context is everything required to bring the content to life and make the event happen.

Contextual issues include: venues or locations; finances; the event's scale and complexity; whether it's a public or private sector event; whether the event has the green light or opposition; technical, logistics and operations; marketing and sponsorship requirements.

Event/Live Event:

Any planned occurrence in real time, for example festivals, guerrilla marketing, major events, mega events, public events, performance art, exhibitions, sports events, demonstrations, live communication, e-sports events, PR stunts, summits, expos, protocol events, field marketing, tradeshows, conferences, seminars, congresses, mass-participation events, conventions, parties, concerts, award shows, fundraisers, theatre, expos, sponsor pavilions, expo pavilions, political rallies, weddings, pop-up events, brand experiences, experiential marketing, cultural events, ceremonies...the list is endless.

I include exhibitions in this list, even though they are sometimes considered by some to be different beasts to events. Throughout this book, if you see the word 'event' you can, if you wish, read the word as 'exhibition'. I don't discriminate between the two.

I'm often asked why I use the term 'live event' rather than just 'event'. Events come in many types and forms, but the one thing they all have in common is that they are live. However, you can call your event or activity whatever you like.

Producing: The act (or craft) of coming up with the idea for, developing, planning, delivering and managing a live event. Producing can, for example, be done by an agency working on behalf of a client, a client's in-house team doing it themselves, an organising committee producing a major event, or an artist creating and developing their own performance in a public space.

Promoter: An individual or company to whom you sell or award the commercial rights of your event so they can exploit those rights to create profit for themselves and in return deliver your event, to the agreed terms, at no cost or less cost to you. They exploit the rights by selling tickets, sponsorship, media rights, or similar.

Some companies may act as both an agency and promoter. While these terms are often confused or regarded as interchangeable, they involve entirely different skillsets and services. We will cover this topic in more detail later in the book.

Stakeholder: A person or organisation integral to a live event. Stakeholders may include someone funding an event, local authorities responsible for providing approvals, or a board or governance body that needs to approve any content or activity. Without the support or permission of these key people, it will be either impossible or extremely difficult to deliver a live event.

Live events are an art and science –
the art of manipulating emotions
and the science of controlling
your own emotions to do so.

Introduction

I wrote this book to create something unique and valuable, something that would, for the first time, address many critical yet often overlooked or unknown facts and insights. Information for those who want to engage with live event professionals, engage with the event industry or for those within the industry already to use if they are looking to improve or develop how they work.

Live events engage audiences by tapping into a whole range of their emotions. Creating live events typically sees creativity, politics and practicalities coupled with immovable deadlines and changing requirements, which can play havoc with logic and the emotions of those involved.

I start by looking at how I ended up in the world of live events and what excites me about them, at how I learned my craft, and at the patterns, trends and common struggles that I came to recognise do no one any favours. We then look at how I set about harnessing the art and science of live events to develop powerful new ideas, extract greater value and create the biggest impact possible – all of which starts at the beginning, with the genesis of a live event and the foundations and key principles that underpin it: The Facts Of Live.

Live events

Art is just art, sport just sport, a message just a message, products just products and music mere music – until you add an audience. With an audience, it doesn't matter what business you think you're in, you're now most definitely in the business of theatre. You're putting on a show and engaging people with a live event, exhibition, pavilion (a semi-permanent building to house events and exhibitions) or similar; you're trying to sell, communicate or entertain, or perhaps all three.

Theatre has evolved over millennia, but it is as powerful in the instant-must-have-it-now world we live in today as it was in Ancient Egypt, at the time of the earliest recorded theatrical event in approximately 2000 BC. Even in the age of digital advancement and our small-screen window on the world, live events are increasingly important as brands, organisations and artists look for meaningful real-life connection and engagement with their customers and audiences.

Events come in many flavours. All events are different, but regardless of scale, type or purpose, at their core they have more elements in common than elements that differentiate them. In every instance, if you're producing a live event, you're producing a piece of theatre. You have a performance space of some sort; you need something engaging in that space; and you have an audience of people whom you want to do or feel something.

Compare the business of events, or theatre, with the construction business for a moment. Architects and engineers follow a core set of principles and practices, irrespective of the scale, type or purpose of the building they are producing. As a result, if someone wants a fabulous building, fit for purpose and likely to stay standing, they need an architect and engineers, even if they don't know what these people do exactly.

Of course, without any experience or qualifications, anyone can go to a hardware store, buy some materials and attempt to build a house, with variable results. But most people who want a house built will engage professionals, and they will know, in broad terms, who those professionals are.

Similarly, events can be produced by people with little or no prior experience. Again, though, the results will vary. Anyone wanting to be sure their event will be fabulous, fit for purpose, and likely to deliver spectacular results needs professionals. By 'professionals', I mean people with relevant qualifications or experience; experts in their craft who can utilise their skills with confidence, clarity and certainty, whether they are paid, volunteers or anywhere in between. Yet where do people, or clients, looking to create a live event find those professionals? What do they do?

If I were to ask 100 people what they would do or where they would turn to commission or produce an event, I would get 100 different answers.

Answers like:

- I'd talk to our marketing department
- I'd find a producer
- I'd talk to my promoter
- I'd talk to procurement
- There's a separate branch of government that deal with that sort of thing
- We'd find an event agency
- We'd find a production company
- We'd find a marketing, advertising or PR agency
- I've no idea so I'd put a committee together
- Mark is super-organised, I'll ask him
- My PA will do that
- We'd ask a consultancy firm to advise us
- We have some event agencies on a framework agreement
- I'd ask you Will (thanks!)
- I'd set up a separate company to do that
- We'd commission a feasibility study

The list is endless.

Unlike other sectors, for example the construction business, there is no obvious, accepted or typical route forward when it comes to commissioning or producing live events. People tend to make it up, guess, do what they've always done, or hope for the best. But if you carry on doing the same thing for decades or only see what happens within your own sector or field of view, how do you really know what's best? As the cliché says, 'You don't know what you don't know.'

People, organisations or agencies who want to create or improve their own professional live event teams, or who want to commission live events in the most powerful, valuable and risk-free way possible to create the biggest impact they can, need a reference point: a set of principles or foundations. As *The Facts Of Live* will explore, your actions and the decisions you make can have a far greater impact on your live

events than those of whomever you bring on board or outsource to. But with no common approach or understanding, how do you know what you're doing is the best approach? Are you relying on word of mouth? Are you relying on your experience of having done an event before? Are you relying on your experience within a specific sector? Are you assuming the approach you've always taken will yield the best results? Are you relying on hearsay?

If you are considering how best to commission or produce a live event, the insights in *The Facts Of Live* will also help you judge whether keeping everything in house with a new or existing team, outsourcing everything, or going for something in between the two is the most appropriate approach.

Having spent twenty years watching and fixing unnecessary struggles, I had to write this book. I have commissioned and produced events of almost every size, shape and form across the globe in both the public and private sectors. I've been involved with and responsible for some of the most ambitious and complex live events, marketing campaigns, sporting events, military pageantry, not-for-profit ventures, cultural festivals and entertainment in recent history, working with global brands and world leaders through to event owners and organising committees. I've worked for, run and built my own successful companies. I've worked client-side, agency-side, and most places in between. I've wrestled with tiny budgets, Mother Nature and terrorist threats, all in the pursuit of creating great events. This variety and depth of experience has given me a possibly unique, certainly hard-earned view across the full gamut of live event activity, practices and perspectives. It has also proven, time and time again, that the way in which events are commissioned and produced is occasionally fabulous, but most of the time it's arduous and often plain broken.

Do any of these sound familiar or worry you?

- Poor creativity, ideas getting watered down, lack of innovation, or wondering where or how to find the best creative talent or ideas

- Trying to wrestle a budget into shape or wrestle with costs as a live event constantly changes and evolves, without knowing or having enough information to forecast expenditure accurately

- Struggling to work out how to procure or contract event-related agencies, goods or services, perhaps without knowing what you want or need, then having to deal with continual changes

- Facing difficulty or confusion in creating or finding the right talent, team or organisation to work on or produce an event, either within your own organisation or with a third party like an event agency or similar

- Trying to wrestle a bewildering number of different stakeholders and organisations into shape against constantly evolving expectations

- Attempting to minimise the physical, financial or reputational risks while not being fully in control

All of these issues are common, and they can turn what should be an exciting and energising project into a feat of endurance. And they can all be avoided or mitigated.

It's no great surprise these issues occur; events are unique beasts, after all. You have a myriad of ideas, people and organisations to glue together seamlessly, often with rapidly changing requirements and typically to an immovable deadline, without being in complete control of everything affecting your success, and you have to deal with all this while everyone is watching. Basically, you're completely exposed.

It can seem like a dark art, but it needn't be so. As I have experienced time and time again, there are some things that don't work at all, some that kind of work, and some that work well. Based on centuries-old theatrical principles coupled with techniques I have developed through my experience of working across multiple sectors, *The Facts Of Live* offers a proven, straightforward approach to commissioning or setting up, managing and improving a professional team to produce powerful events of any scale, whether this is your first time or you have been in this world for decades. Rather than offering an education on how to produce an entire event, this book assumes you primarily want to work with or already have a team of professionals.

Whether you're in the sport, entertainment, arts, marketing, communication, government or not-for-profit business, if you want to extract the most value and create the maximum impact using live events while also enjoying the experience, it all starts with *The Facts Of Live*.

My history with live events

I still remember it clearly now. I was at university, looking down from a balcony at a thousand or so people enjoying themselves, bouncing up and down and dancing around at an event I had just produced. The wave of adrenaline that rushed through me was immense. I was hooked.

For some of us, live events are like an addiction. There's the anticipation: the designing, development and planning. Then the adrenaline rush at seeing an event we've produced play out live. There are the emotions an audience experiences due to how we've crafted the content to manipulate their senses, and there are the often powerful emotions we feel ourselves – emotions caused by how raw and real live events are to produce. Then there's the comedown as the adrenaline subsides, followed by the hunt for the next adrenaline hit; the anticipation of the next live event. It really is success or failure; there's nowhere in between and nowhere to hide.

When I compare it to my achievements later in life, the scale of the first event I produced at university was tiny. Yet, to this day, it remains one of my proudest achievements. Written off academically at one point, I still managed, somehow, to get into one of the UK's best universities. Once there, struggling to find any enthusiasm for the degree I was supposed to be studying for, I decided I was going to produce the university's biggest event ever.

Even though much of my final year at university was spent producing this event rather than studying, I managed to leave with a degree. More importantly, though, I had found an outlet for my creativity and a use for my tenacity to drive things forward: live events.

I assumed not all the people who produced live events in the real world started off at university, trying to avoid studying as enthusiastically as I was. I assumed, too, that people must get paid for doing such things. After a quick bit of research had proven both these assumptions to be correct, I decided I wanted to learn the many crafts involved in producing events, some artistic, some commercial, some technical and some practical, and I wanted to learn from the best. I knew that one day I wanted to create amazing live events, and to do so with gravitas and authority, I would learn the principles of all the crafts involved by working on the front line. If I was going to lead people, I was going to make sure I knew exactly how to do the things I'd be asking them to do.

Despite the odds, by channelling every bit of my tenacity, staying just on the right side of becoming irritating, I landed my first proper job after leaving university with a company called Imagination, one of the largest and most respected design and event agencies on the planet. Eight years later, having worked in a vast number of countries and been involved with huge and ambitious events for some of the best-known blue chip brands in the world, I had completed what I still consider to be

my apprenticeship. I had worked on events ranging from bold to beautiful and everything in between, delivered events that were so huge they needed new roads, buildings and technical infrastructure, developed niche theatrical productions, and travelled the world, often trying to make amazing things happen to the highest standards against ever-increasing obstacles. I had learned the craft I was looking to learn from people many considered to be the best in the world. It was comparable to learning to be an architect under the guidance of Richard Rogers or the late Zaha Hadid, or training to be a chef with Gordon Ramsay or Heston Blumenthal.

During this first decade of my career, a train of thought that wouldn't go away started to form in my mind. It always struck me that producing events seemed to be a lot more complicated than it needed to be, both for the clients and those they had commissioned to produce their events. I couldn't put my finger on why though, or whether there was an alternative, so at the time, it was just a nagging hunch.

With my almost decade-long apprenticeship complete, it was time to step out into the big, wide and unsupported world. I joined a smaller company than Imagination, a marketing and events agency that showed great promise, becoming its managing director as the company went from strength to strength, often punching well above its weight. An advantage of being at the sharp end of a company was that it exposed me to the business side of things rather than just the craft of creating a live event. I soon understood, intimately, the sometimes harsh commercial realities of live events.

After almost three incredibly productive and successful years, I was convinced I had considerably more to offer and wanted to work for myself. I also felt ready. Having worked from the ground up, learning both the craft and the business, I decided I was qualified to speak and advise with

authority. I also had a diverse variety of credible, demonstrable world-class experience behind me.

At this stage of my career, I was still regularly witnessing the confusing approach many organisations adopted when they commissioned events, and the sometimes counterintuitive approach many agencies and those producing their own events in house seemed to adopt, too. An event's impact will be less than it could be when talented people become swallowed up in wrestling with politics, processes and contracts rather than plying their craft. The impact is often then further diminished by a vast proportion of the budget being spent on unnecessary bureaucracy. Practices that work in other sectors clearly don't work for live events, and a general lack of knowledge and insight often leads to poor commercial decisions and practices.

By their very nature, live events leave you exposed. You're on show. Therefore, they can be seen as high risk financially, operationally and reputationally. All of these risks are manageable, yet they are so often left to chance or mitigated with contracts. But contracts are, practically speaking, an ineffectual approach given that once a live event is live, it's happening. There is little to no time to consult a contract to assign blame or resolve a situation.

These issues and more, coupled with the fact that an event deadline is typically immovable, add increasing pressure on all parties involved. In turn, stress, confusion and frustration can increase, resulting in the wrong sort of hard work. The often inevitable politics and egos involved in live events, if left unmanaged, can lead to logic and common sense giving way to panic. Rather than a live event being the enjoyable experience for all involved that it should be, it becomes a chore.

Even though these issues were clear to me, I didn't have a plan. I didn't yet know how to solve the problems I was seeing, but I knew live events needed a different approach, and I knew I wanted to work with and help people across the event spectrum. Full of enthusiasm, off the back of being offered a major government event contract by people who knew something needed to change and had the courage to put their faith in me to make it happen, in 2008, I went into business myself. That was it: I was off.

I spent the next ten years working with, and still work with, clients, agencies, suppliers, governments, rights holders, organising committees and individuals, applying the science I had developed to tame and direct the emotions, politics, egos, chaos and uncertainty inherent in producing live events more productively and effectively. I work on everything from sports and arts events to helping cities bid for major events, developing new event businesses and designing venues and spaces with architects and developers. I also enjoy working with companies that exist solely to create and produce their own events, selling directly to consumers, audiences or participants. I've helped brands such as Coke, Samsung and UEFA along with world leaders, had my work praised in Parliament (UK Government), become an author and speaker, and featured in print, on TV and radio, all while developing a possibly unique view across the entire event spectrum, and a deep understanding and empathy with all parties involved.

The reason I have waited until now to write this book is that I wanted to be sure I had proven solutions. Opinions are easy to find; everyone has them. *The Facts Of Live* represents the result of years of research and experience on the front line across different sectors.

For a long time, I was convinced I needed to focus on the event industry and its practices. I have gradually realised, though, that the issues that exist are not entirely solvable by the event industry. Many issues come about as a result of how those who commission events or seek event services engage with event companies and those with event expertise, and then, in turn, how the event industry ties itself in knots in order to respond and operate in the awkward manner clients request. It's a perfect storm; it's also completely understandable. Unlike so many other industries or sectors, there are no common or accepted guidelines to commissioning or producing live events. As a result, every client or organisation approaches its live events in a slightly different way. The industry then has to respond in a different way to every client or for every event. By the time a client and the experts they've chosen are working together, they've often already set an irreversible path in motion. This path is generally inefficient, leads to huge complexity and confusion, and can limit an event's potential.

All of this is avoidable.

Common struggles

Through all of my work, I witness clients, agencies, governments and organising committees etc wrestling with the same unnecessary issues time and time again. I see creativity becoming watered down and organisations struggling to find the best, right or new ideas. Organisations, brands and agencies trying to glue together various creative disciplines effectively seems to be a common issue, too.

Clients often tie themselves in knots working out how best to procure events and event services. Given that most events evolve as a partnership between the client and an agency, companies try to find awkward ways around their own, rightly rigid, internal procurement governance and guidelines to accommodate fluid and often non-rigid and indefinable event services and requirements. It's easy to see why this is a problem – after all, how do you define or specify an event sufficiently as part of a procurement process if the purpose of procuring an agency or similar is to develop that event with you? You often need the expertise you're procuring in order to work out how to procure what you need.

I frequently see clients argue and agonise over cents and pennies, when a simple change in structure or approach could save them thousands, hundreds of thousands or even millions. Yet, with a preference for the status quo, people on all sides carry on regardless, either through ignorance or fear of reprisal. I also see agencies spending time managing contracts, procurement issues and confusing information rather than focusing on producing a great event. All of this, whether they realise it or not, costs both the agency and its client time and money.

I've regularly watched organisations, clients and agencies put teams together or try to manage teams that are inappropriately structured for the task in hand. The teams are often structured to mirror antiquated internal practices or marry up with internal client or stakeholder expectations or structures rather than what's best for the live event. Strangely, team structure is often one of the last things clients and agencies consider when they are wondering if there could be a better way to create a live event, or why they are facing confusion, unnecessary complexity, cost-control issues, creative issues etc. That is, if it gets considered at all. More often than not, people just accept the existing team as part of the game, which I've always found strange.

It is not uncommon, either, for clients to approach those with relevant content experience to lead things or head up event-related ventures, for example a sportsperson to lead the development of a sporting event, a marketing professional to lead the development of a brand's event, or an artist to lead the creation of an artistic event. Of course these people need to be involved, and early on, they may even be the public figurehead of the event, but unless they have prior experience of doing so, they are no more qualified to produce an event than a nurse is to be the architect of a hospital.

This is not to say everything is doom and gloom. Far from it. People being people, they find a way around everything. Sometimes the adversity and challenges even make a team stronger and more determined, even if these challenges are, obviously or otherwise, self-inflicted. Yet when people and companies are struggling unnecessarily, wasting money, feeling frustrated, producing average rather than great results, not living up to their potential, not enjoying the process, I find it difficult not to step in.

Live events are incredibly exciting. I love creating them and working with them, no matter how large or small they are. It is, though, necessary to get the foundations right first rather than glossing over them and moving on to the exciting stuff – yes, even I have been guilty of this on occasion. Discipline is essential.

Most problems and frustrations I see typically fall into one of three broad categories: creativity and content, procurement and contracting, or technical and operational issues.

Creative and content. Creative and content issues affect the purpose or design of an event, and the development and nurturing of ideas, for example:

- How a brand presents its message, content or products
- How a brand designs or creates an exhibition or PR stunt
- How a brand develops an event strategy or harnesses consumer insights
- How a brand or country finds the right design for a sponsorship or expo pavilion
- How a sporting event dresses up and presents sporting action
- How an artist brings their art to life
- How a government hosts international visitors at a summit

or gets a message across to the people it represents

The Facts Of Live will show you the best way to go about finding and delivering the right ideas, innovations or creativity, making sure they don't get watered down. It will do this by looking at how to glue together and lead the various creative skillsets required.

Procurement and contracting. Whatever your involvement with the event industry may be, *The Facts Of Live* will provide a clear, proven approach to procuring event services (creative solutions, management or delivery personnel, for example) or goods, simply and effectively. This approach accommodates the necessary and uniquely symbiotic relationship commissioning and producing events demands of parties on both sides of any contract.

The Facts Of Live will look at how to get what you need when you need it, possibly even before you know exactly what you need. It provides guidance on how to consider budgets, quotes and costs with more certainty and control, looking at how to minimise financial, physical and reputational concerns and risk.

Technical and operational. *The Facts Of Live* provides a clear blueprint for the most effective team structures, irrespective of whether they're within an organisation (a brand, government or arts company, for example), an event agency, an organising committee, or anywhere else among any combination of people or organisations involved with a live event. It will look at the fundamental mindset and approaches that you need to make sure are in place and understood in order to keep events on track, increasing their impact and value while reducing risk.

I realise there are a great many other considerations and functions frequently associated with events, for example: funding and sponsorship, sales, marketing, environmental and sustainability concerns, and safety issues to name just a few. These, though, are separate disciplines and industries in their own right with a plentiful supply of books, courses, training, experts and advice covering them already.

You can also already find advice on and training for event management and all the individual elements of it – ticketing, hospitality, lighting, sound, staging and design etc – in abundance.

The Facts Of Live is about getting the foundations right. All the other functions, services and expertise can then follow.

An almost impossible book

This book nearly never saw the light of day as it's a book I found difficult to write. So much of what I am involved with is inherently public, yet behind the scenes, almost everything that brings live events into the public eye is extremely confidential. By the very nature of what I do, reputation and confidentiality are, to a certain extent, my lifeblood.

This makes discussing anything I've done tricky. In writing *The Facts Of Live*, I wanted neither to betray any confidences nor to risk having any points of view misconstrued. Those who know me well know my heart is always in the right place; those who don't, please understand that all the points of view in this book come from me wanting to help – something I do day in, day out. I have anonymised most examples I have used throughout the book and changed names and certain details to honour confidentiality. To that end, I would ask you to focus on the underlying message in any case studies and examples, rather than on the accuracy of specific names or inferred types of events, which have been altered.

Firm foundations

Someone once introduced me as I was about to walk on to stage to give a talk as 'the expert the experts turn to'. My ego certainly liked the introduction, so perhaps inevitably, the phrase stuck. And it's this expertise that I wish to share in *The Facts Of Live* – expertise that I will always continue to improve and develop by working with individuals and organisations to create live events with ever greater impact and value.

The proven foundations you will discover throughout the pages of *The Facts Of Live*, all based on real-world experience and hard-earned expertise, will serve as an authoritative and definitive reference point, demonstrating how to couple the science necessary to harness the emotions involved in producing a live event with the art of manipulating the senses to generate powerful emotional responses in your audience. This reference point is specifically for:

- People or organisations looking to build their own professional event, or in-house exhibition teams, or an organising committee
- People or organisations looking to improve how they or their teams produce events or exhibitions professionally
- People or organisations looking to commission (outsource) an event, exhibition or pavilion, either partly or in its entirety
- Agencies looking to improve how they produce events and exhibitions

To accompany this book, www.TheFactsOfLive.com also serves as a quick reference guide complete with further insights and updates.

Now let's examine what a live event is exactly. What value does it bring? What is the point of any live event? And why are they so powerful?

1

If you leave your audience moved, a live event is the most powerful medium you have to sell, communicate or entertain.

Chapter 1

The Purpose Of Live Events

This chapter addresses the purpose of live events; what they're best used for and their value, what they're perhaps best not used for, what makes them so powerful and their place and relevance in an increasingly digital world.

With so many different sectors merging and live events having an increasing number of demands upon them to be more things to more people, we look at how a universal approach to creating and producing live events or a universal understanding at least can benefit everyone.

The only three things you can do with a live event

A live event's purpose will be one, two or all three of these things: to sell something, to communicate something, or to entertain.

Selling is vividly explaining, demonstrating, promoting or having people experience the benefits of your product, service, destination or other offering. Examples of selling include a brand offering an experiential marketing event, tradeshows demonstrating products and services within a particular sector, a major sporting event being used to promote a city to a worldwide audience, field marketing offering consumers the chance to sample products, seminars selling information or training, or an auction selling products to the highest bidder.

Communicating in this context is delivering a message to an audience in the most powerful way possible. Examples include a conference with speakers articulating their points of view, a brand's senior management addressing staff at an internal communications conference, a wedding where a couple announce their commitment publicly to friends and family, a government conference explaining policy change, a pastor addressing their congregation, or a large population staging a demonstration or political rally.

Entertaining could be a band or musician performing live, a sporting activity put on in front of a live audience, a theatrical performance, a mass-participation sporting event for the public to enjoy (or endure!), an artist delivering their art on the street, a poet or comedian performing in front of their audience, or a music festival.

Many events aim to be and do more than one thing. Sporting events, for example, often encompass all three of selling, communicating and entertaining. While an audience is being entertained by the sport happening, a major sporting event will more often than not be dominated by sales and communication efforts promoting the sport, the city or country it's hosted in, and the brands that sponsor it. As sports compete to capture audience share, the sporting action itself is presented in ever more innovative guises, enhancing the spectators' experience to seek deeper engagement.

Similarly, a performing artist, be they a singer on stage, a street performer or a magician in a theatre, is rarely just entertaining. They have music they want their audience to download or buy, they have merchandise to sell, they've sold tickets to attend the event in the first place, and they may have brands sponsoring them that they want their audience to engage with. Many artists also have views and opinions they wish to share with their audiences or causes important to them, making their events powerful communication tools.

Art in front of an audience is entertainment; engagement; show business; theatre – whatever you call it, once it has a live audience, it becomes a live event.

Brands, governments and not-for-profits looking to communicate and engage with their audience, be it other businesses or consumers, use events such as exhibition stands, experiential marketing initiatives, product launches, award shows, annual general meetings or shareholder meetings to engage in selling, communicating and entertaining in one hit, sometimes obviously, sometimes less so. Brands' event activities are typically a combination of communication to get their key messages, values, issues and plans across, entertainment to keep their audience engaged, and selling because brands usually need to sell something to stay alive.

Value of live events

An event's purpose should provide value, so the cost and effort required to produce an event often give rise to conversations around its value.

While the investment you need to produce a great event needn't be hugely disproportionate to the return that's likely on that investment, if return on investment is important to you, as it is to most people, then clearly you need to make a value judgment. If money or budget is less important to you, then the cost or value of a live event will be a far lesser concern. There are, though, many events that happen that clearly offer at best very little value and at worst none at all. These events tend to fall into three categories.

First are the events that get produced and delivered for no other reason than tradition. Whenever anyone questions the purpose of these events, the organisers' response is usually, 'Well, we've always done it, so we're doing it again.' If a traditional event offers some value, even if it's only a welcome distraction from the norm, then it arguably has some merit. Yet if the event serves no one, is stale or no one really cares about it, then its existence needs challenging in my view.

Typical examples of tradition-led events are internal communications meetings that do little to inspire or communicate, held only because a team has been told to hold them, or vanity events where products or people are rolled out just for the sake of it without any benefit to the brand or audience, and without engaging the media or marketing channels in any meaningful way.

The second type of event that offers little or no value is the event that is completely ineffectual. There is little point, for example, inviting an audience to a conference to listen to someone speaking on stage and to watch a few films if there are no opportunities for the audience to network or interact at the conference. Unless the person on stage is a celebrity or someone the audience just wants to be in the same room as, which will be valuable to some, there are far cheaper, quicker and more engaging ways of delivering content digitally. I admit I am a tough audience, but I am sure we have all at one time or another politely endured an event while wondering what the point of being there is, especially if we could have spent that time at home with our feet up on the sofa, watching the same content on our phones while devouring a tub of ice cream!

Finally, there are events that needn't be events, which are perhaps the most common examples of poor value events. The best example of this is an event staged simply to capture a photo or piece of video content. In these cases, it's a photoshoot or film shoot you need, which will produce the same result for considerably less money.

In a similar vein, if you hope to get your audience trying or experiencing your product or service, but the cost of an event to do this outweighs the cost of simply buying or supplying the relevant number of products to your target audience size, then there is little commercial point to producing the event. Yet in my experience, it is surprising how many people ignore this simple piece of maths.

Charity events deserve a special mention. While many charity events do more than just raise money, whether it's a participatory sporting event, a black-tie fundraising gala dinner or anything in between, I am often astonished by the amount of money organisers are willing to spend on such events. In some cases, it would be more beneficial either to donate the money to the charity or to have those paying to attend or take part donate their ticket price or entry fee to charity.

Providing your event or event idea passes a quick and honest appraisal to ensure it doesn't fall into the tradition, ineffectual or non-event categories outlined above, there is no reason why it will be anything other than good value – provided you don't spend more than you need to, of course. We'll get to that later.

Power of live events

There is plenty of scientific evidence to prove that experiencing something live is the best way to learn or understand. Moreover, offering an audience the opportunity to experience something live is the most powerful form of communication. This is why we choose to go and see our favourite musicians perform live, why we go to our friends' weddings rather than just look at the photos, and why we want to be in the stadium to watch the match or the athletics final. Live events are real, raw and emotive. Little else can compare.

One could argue, as I would, that in an increasingly digital world, awareness is relatively simple and cheap to achieve. Real connection, emotional engagement and impact is where live events will always triumph and be most powerful. Are you more likely to understand how to use something new if it is demonstrated to you and you're able to touch or feel it? Are you more likely to enjoy music live rather than listening to it through a stereo or headphones? Are you more likely to enjoy or get the benefit from an activity by participating in it rather than watching it? Are you more likely to believe someone if they are standing in front of you, talking to you and engaging with you rather than just posting on social media? Of course, so long as you believe them to be authentic, which is much easier to determine if they are in front of you.

Imagine watching a 100m running final alone without 50,000 other people in the stadium creating an electrifying atmosphere. Imagine watching a speech on your phone rather than hearing it live and being able to interact with the speaker on stage or see how a large audience reacts to them. The power of a shared experience is difficult to achieve with anything other than a live event. Whether two people are sharing an idea or a crowd of 100,000 is watching a performance on stage, the power and energy they will experience by sharing the same moment is both impossible to measure and impossible to ignore. Never underestimate the effect this has in amplifying a sales pitch, message or performance. Live events are real, raw and unfiltered, reaching all of an audience's senses simultaneously. It's this multi-sensory experience that makes them so powerful.

Harness the power of live events to leave your audience feeling moved emotionally – moved to buy more of your stuff if you're selling something; moved to think differently or understand you if you're trying to communicate something; moved by incredible entertainment if you're in the entertainment game. If you don't leave your audience, spectators or participants moved, your live event has little point and will offer little value to either you or your audience.

Live experiences in a digital world

It is worth touching upon how the power of live events fits into a world where there are so many channels and media to choose from, many of them digital.

Electronic devices are increasingly governing our lives. There is only so much connection such a device can offer, though. As part of an integrated marketing and communication strategy, nothing is going to compete with the internet and digital platforms when it comes to getting your message out there. They will be the quickest, cheapest and most effective method to distribute content and build awareness of your brand, message, product or service. Whether your audience is super niche, hyperlocal, or the entire global population, there are digital tools that will distribute your message far more efficiently than any event will. If this is your sole aim, there is little to no point staging an event.

If, though, you want your customers or audience to experience, touch and feel your products or services, if you want your audience to hear your message from you or your people face to face, if you want to build strong, powerful personal relationships or if you want to entertain people, it is hard to match a live event. A live event can also act as a powerful catalyst at a moment in time to drive traffic and engagement across digital channels. If your digital audience shares or interacts with your live event and the content it produces in real time, this amplifies the event's power and potential. Live events are becoming as much about providing material for audiences watching on social media and digital channels as the audiences physically at the events.

There is undoubtedly a continual drive to find ways of bringing the real world to life on digital media, from augmented reality to virtual reality.

These all have a place in the modern world and will, I am sure, continue to evolve until all five of our senses can't tell the difference between what is real and what is artificial. This is a few decades away, though, so in the meantime, there is a far more powerful three-dimensional non-virtual reality and experience we can use – it's called a live event.

A universal approach

Regardless of their scale, type or purpose, at a core level, all live events have the same foundations, just as the universal fundamentals or principles of architecture will always apply in the building trade regardless of the type or purpose of that building. However, the method by which an event comes to fruition is often determined by the sector from which it originates. Different sectors have slightly different approaches. Sports event organisers tend to split the production of the event down into numerous departments, with committees and sub-committees running different work streams and 'functional areas' of activity in parallel. Brand events, be they for corporates, government or not-for-profit brands, tend to adopt a top down approach with all activity led from a central point. Exhibitions and pavilions can often be treated more as shopfitting or architectural exercises rather than live events as such.

These are just a handful of examples to illustrate my point and they are generalisations; there are, of course, exceptions. With so many different practices and approaches to organising a live event, what elements of each approach work best? And perhaps more importantly, as sectors continue to evolve and merge, finding ever more interesting and innovative ways of collaborating, and events become increasingly hard to place in any one particular sector, would an approach that works for any event, regardless of its type, scale or purpose, be better for everyone? For example, sporting events now are not just about sport, but also about entertainment and the activities of the brands that sponsor the sport, so which sector's approach should the organisers adopt? As our world and markets evolve, I believe that a universal approach to live events, or at least a universal understanding of them, has never been more important.

Summary

In this chapter, we have examined the purpose and power of live events, detailing the only three things we can use them for: to sell something, to communicate something and/or to entertain.

We have talked about the value a live event can have, looking at the three types of events that offer little to no return on investment: the traditional event that's only delivered because it's always been delivered, regardless of whether it's still effective or relevant; the ineffectual event which leaves the audience wondering why they bothered turning up at all; and the non-event, for example an event to run alongside a photoshoot, the photoshoot being the essential task and the event completely surplus to requirements.

We have talked about the power of a live event to educate and communicate to our audiences, and how we can work with the ever-increasing digital channels to enhance that power.

In order to make sure a live event has the maximum impact, we need a set of foundations, a common route to success that will work for any live event, regardless of its size, and regardless of the sector it sits within.

Brands exhibiting their wares at exhibitions are constantly striving to stand out from others, attract audiences and engage with those audiences, leading to the adoption of new ideas and concepts. As they try to find interesting ways to engage other businesses or consumers, they are increasingly using sport, the arts and entertainment to differentiate themselves.

The arts and entertainment sectors are frequently looking to find new revenue streams and opportunities, meaning they may want to work with brands and organisations across various sectors. Not-for-profit organisations face incredible pressures and competition, meaning they too are looking at partnerships and opportunities within other sectors.

As all these sectors and the people within them converge, traditional boundaries are becoming increasingly blurred. Live events are becoming less easy to identify as just sporting events, arts events, entertainment events or brand experiences, for example. More and more, they are simply 'live events'.

Whether you will be using them yourself or ensuring those you bring on board adopt them, the set of universal principles you will discover in the pages of *The Facts Of Live*

will ground any live event with firm foundations, regardless of its scale, type or purpose, and underpin all activity as work progresses to create the maximum value and impact possible. Any set of universal principles is based on commonality, and the main commonality between all live events is, of course, that you are on show. You're on a stage and you have an audience. You're producing theatre, one of the oldest art forms in the world.

How does theatre work, though?

2

No two live events are the same, yet all live events have identical anatomies.

Chapter 2

The Anatomy Of Live Events

Here we analyse the unique environment live events exist in: constantly changing requirements, a fixed deadline, everyone watching you and how you or those you bring on board are rarely able to fully control everything affecting your success.

We outline the important differences between content and context, content being the purpose of a live event, context being everything required to deliver the content – the context in or against which the content is created and delivered.

We look at how theatrical principles and four key roles can be used as the backbone to any live event, of any type, of any scale and for any purpose.

The theatre of live events

Live events evolve in a unique set of circumstances. You, or those you bring on board, find yourself having to glue together an often bewildering number of issues, people and organisations against a constantly changing backdrop. You never really have complete control over certain elements that can contribute towards your success. The public, weather, people changing their minds, egos, politics and more can, and will, affect your event. You are completely exposed; everyone is watching and many are judging. To top all of this off, you typically have a deadline that cannot be moved.

Sounds fun, doesn't it? These are some formidable obstacles.

Commissioning, creating, managing or producing anything live is quite unlike pursuits in other fields. Even live television affords you the luxury of being able to cut away to another camera or pre-recorded video. In truth, the only other industries dealing with a similar it-must-happen-now-come-what-may approach are the emergency or medical services and the military. They have to do something at a particular time, regardless of what's going on around them. Whatever they are doing is the only thing that matters at that point in time.

It's perhaps no coincidence that both the room in which a surgeon operates and a war zone are known as theatres. And the skills required in the creation and delivery of live events have their roots in theatre, too.

Against a unique backdrop, live events need approaching differently to other pursuits. The speed of their organisation, immovable deadlines, and often uncontrollable curveballs coupled with limited resources mean typical project management techniques can fail and people can react erratically to the pressures that arise. An additional pressure is the challenge of marrying the flexible and unpredictable world of live events with the typically inflexible, risk-averse and certainty-seeking world most people and organisations operate within. This wild marriage of the inflexible and flexible can lead to a special and unique sort of excitement, but it is also a relationship that, with some different thinking, empathy and a few key principles, can be tamed.

Content and context

There can't be many types of live event that I've not been involved with in one way or another. Regardless of type, location, sector, scale or purpose, there are two fundamental parts of any live event: content and context. These are two words I use often, so you need to understand them fully in relation to live events, whether you're looking to outsource your live event requirements or build or improve your own team.

In the Glossary, I outlined the important differences between content and context, **content** being the purpose of a live event, **context** being everything required to deliver the content. In other words, we're talking about the context in or against which the content is created and delivered. Figure 2.1 details four different examples of live events to illustrate this.

Firstly, a sporting event. The content is the sport itself: the athletes or participants, the equipment they need, and the rules they abide by.

The contextual issues are numerous. The finances involved: what the event generates (revenues) and what it costs to stage. The venue or location the sporting event will happen in. The marketing: how it will attract spectators or sell tickets. The complexity of the event is a key contextual issue. The technical and infrastructure requirements, often referred to as 'overlay' in sporting circles. The logistics and operations to move, accommodate, feed and look after the competitors, spectators and everyone else involved. The scale of the event and the size of the team to cover the work required to bring it to fruition.

Next, let's look at a popular music event: a concert, perhaps. The content is the singer, the band and their material, along with their performance. This is the purpose of the concert.

The contextual issues are finance, marketing, the venue or location, the scale or complexity of the event, the technical and infrastructure requirements, the logistics and

Content and Context Differences

Event Type	Content	Context
Sporting Event	Athletes, participants, sporting equipment, competition or sporting rules and sport-specific requirements.	Finances, venue, location, marketing, scale, complexity, infrastructure, technology, logistics, operations, travel, accommodation, catering and similar.
Concert	Artists or performers and their material along with their performances.	Finances, venue, location, marketing, scale, complexity, infrastructure, technology, logistics, operations, travel, accommodation, catering and similar.
Conference	Speakers on stage, their material, any activities and the conference's message or purpose.	Finances, venue, location, marketing, scale, complexity, infrastructure, technology, logistics, operations, travel, accommodation, catering and similar.
Street Theatre	The art, performances and performers along with the message, meaning or purpose of the performance.	Finances, venue, location, marketing, scale, complexity, infrastructure, technology, logistics, operations, travel, accommodation, catering and similar.

Figure 2.1: Content and context differences

operational factors, and the size of the team involved.

On a more corporate note, let's take a look at a conference. The content is the speakers on stage, any material they present and/or the message behind the conference. This is the conference's purpose.

The contextual issues are finance, marketing, the venue or location, the scale or complexity of the event, the technical and infrastructure requirements, the logistics and operational factors, and the size of the team involved. Can you see a theme appearing here?

Finally, let's consider some public performance art, perhaps an installation in a public space with dancers performing in and around it. The content is the art itself, and if there are performers or artists involved, they are the content, too.

The contextual issues are, again, finance, any marketing required, the venue or site of the installation, the scale or complexity of the event, the technical and infrastructure requirements, and any necessary logistics or operations.

When we look at them in this way, we can see that all live events share more similarities than differences. A concert for 1,000 people will likely have the same, or similar, content as a concert by the same artist for 100,000 people. It will, however, have completely different contextual considerations. On the other hand, a concert for 100,000 people will have similar contextual considerations as a sporting event for 100,000 spectators, but it will, of course, have completely different content.

An event's content and context can become muddled or blurred as our focus shifts from one to the other, depending on who's involved and what seems most important, or most exciting, at any given time. Decisions regarding something's importance are usually led, wrongly, by whoever's shouting the loudest or using the most capital letters and exclamation marks in their emails.

I have worked with many artistic and creative people who are, rightly, super excited about their art yet switch off immediately when it comes to the contextual issues necessary to bring their art to life. It's not necessary for them to get involved, but it is necessary for them to ensure those details are being dealt with appropriately.

Conversely, I have worked with immensely talented and organised brand and management teams looking to produce a great experiential marketing event, sporting event or product launch, for example. Occasionally, they can, understandably, be so focused on operational details, financial due diligence and box ticking, all of which are also known as the contextual issues, that the content of their event is at best underwhelming, and at worst completely ineffectual. They

don't necessarily need to focus on the content, but they do need to ensure it's being dealt with appropriately. This is critical to the success, and impact, of their event.

Without a proven approach or set of principles that gives appropriate balance to both the content and contextual issues, your live event is never going to have the impact it could otherwise. It will return less value and may be higher risk than it needs to be.

It's always important not to confuse content and contextual experience. A world-class Olympian, despite having participated in many events, doesn't necessarily have the contextual experience to create and lead a live event. An established artist won't necessarily have the relevant contextual experience to deliver their art in a public space. Someone who has for years led and created brand experiences won't necessarily have the relevant content experience to know how to market a product best, nor will someone who's produced great music events necessarily know how to create great music.

This balance between content and context is what separates a great event from one that's merely average. Achieving that balance comes from making sure you have the right team in place, from the outset.

The four key roles

Whether it's Madonna singing in front of a crowd of thousands, Usain Bolt running the 100m final inside a stadium packed with spectators, a CEO addressing her company's shareholders at an AGM, a brand exhibiting their products at an exhibition, or a country demonstrating their culture within a pavilion at an expo, all live events have a stage (or performance area), an audience, and they are live. They are in every sense theatrical performances.

Theatre is an art form that has its origins as far back as Ancient Egyptian times, evidenced by hieroglyphics from this period depicting religious ceremonies with priests wearing animal heads as costumes to impersonate, and presumably worship, their gods. Moving forward a few years, the Ancient Greeks are well known for their theatrical heritage, with performances serving all manner of purposes from entertainment and sport through to religion and politics.

The Romans were partial to a bit of theatre, too. As anyone with even a small amount of historical knowledge, or anyone who's watched Ridley Scott's film *Gladiator*, will know, the participants in some Roman sporting events didn't always fare too well, yet the audience loved the spectacle. Later, medieval times through to the modern day have seen the art form evolve into what people now recognise more traditionally as theatre.

Theatre is both an art and a science, though, and the principles and core roles we require to deliver theatre are similar the world over. All theatrical performances have someone producing them: someone in charge of holding the performance together, driving it forward, finding and managing the money, putting the team together, getting the performance to the opening night and beyond, and making sure it ends up being what it's supposed to be. The producer leads everything: they produce a show. They are the equivalent of a CEO, manging director or similar for the production.

A director directs the performance – the content. They may have an army of writers, choreographers, designers and a musical director to help them, but the director is in charge of the content of the show. They make sure the performance maintains its creative integrity, engages the audience, and they get the best out of the cast, crew and support staff.

A production manager or technical director (they may have any manner of other titles) is responsible for producing and delivering all the technical and physical elements of the show, including, for example, staging, scenery and costumes. Finally, someone, somewhere, will be taking care of all the operational and logistics requirements: welfare, ticketing, catering, accommodation, and front of house (auditorium) requirements.

There will be many more people involved, from accountants and health and safety staff through to designers, stage managers and a company manager, but there will always be a core team that some might call 'senior management'. Four key roles: someone leading; someone in charge of the content; someone to deliver it physically; and someone looking after the operational side of things. These four roles are the backbone of any theatrical performance. They may be covered by four different people with dozens or even hundreds of people reporting in to them; they may all be undertaken by the same person if the performance or location is tiny. However, these four key roles always exist in some way, shape or form. It is these four key roles, and how the content and contextual issues are split between them, that form the foundations of making sure your event creates the most impact and returns the most value while keeping your risks to a minimum.

Your perfectly formed team

Of course, not all live events are held in theatres. All live events, though, have a performance space, content in that performance space, and an audience, meaning the tried and tested approach to producing and delivering theatre is just as relevant for any live event. It's an approach that has been proven time and time again the world over.

We're now going to look at the team of four people, or, more accurately, the four roles you need either to put in place or to make sure someone else puts in place if you are outsourcing your activity, as illustrated in Figure 2.2.

The boundaries between the four key roles can blur, but getting the right team in place and the right marriage between content and context is critical.

In looking at this team, you need to make sure you're clear on the difference between the words 'content' and 'context'. The content

is the purpose of a live event, the context is everything you require to deliver the content.

Key role 1: lead. The first key role is the person who will lead your live event – the producer, if we are using theatre terminology.

Remember, live events have a fixed deadline and everyone is watching. You have to deliver and you have to deliver on time, which requires your producer to glue together all manner of issues, people and organisations. They support the content, but it is not essential that they have experience of the content. It is, however, imperative that the person leading your live event has relevant contextual experience.

For example, in 2009 I was asked to be the event director (the person leading the live event) of the new World Championship Series Triathlon in Central London. I knew nothing about triathlons. I'd never seen one, nor had I ever participated in one. I wasn't even that clear about the order in which the competitors swam, cycled and ran.

The people who decided to ask me to take the role on recognised that I had the contextual experience of leading and delivering a major public event in a major city centre, navigating the politics of a bewildering number of stakeholders who had competing objectives. They recognised that I would be able to ensure the marketing and communication would be appropriate, support various sporting organisations to the level they'd need, and deliver on budget, with a supportive attitude and to a world-class standard. Some people from within the triathlon world did question this decision, given I knew nothing about the sport. My response was to point out that the triathlon expertise would be available in spades. The content of the event, the triathlon, already existed; what the event needed was someone to help the triathlon experts create and deliver the event, driving the project forward, taking everyone with them, and supporting them as it headed towards its immovable deadline.

To give you another example, I was once asked to support or find a replacement for a producer who had produced a small, beautiful and intimate piece of performance art within a theatre. This piece of art was being transferred from the theatre and scaled up to be performed in a large outdoor public space. The content remained largely unchanged, yet the contextual issues were exponentially more complicated. The producer in this instance didn't have the contextual experience to produce the enlarged live event, even though they had previously produced the content many times over.

Event manager, producer, event director, project manager, director, executive producer – whatever term you use to describe your leader, it's the person's contextual experience that matters most. Content knowledge or experience is a bonus; contextual experience is the priority. Look at

Four Key Roles For Any Live Event

| Project or Event Lead | Creative or Content Lead | Production or Technical Lead | Logistics or Operations Lead |

Additional staff, crew, any volunteers, functional areas, departments, stakeholders, contractors (vendors or suppliers) and any other people or organisations involved; all report or link into one or all of the four key roles.

Figure 2.2: Four key roles

your event, and ask if the person you're considering for the role of producer has worked with similar budget levels (be they high or low), marketing requirements, technical requirements, team sizes, scopes, project complexities and locations. Are they capable of leading the live event with the resources available, be they financial resources or personnel? If the person you're considering for this role has led similar live events before with a huge staff supporting them, they won't necessarily have the skillset to do the same with a reduced staff. If they have led similar events before with a small team, will they be able to cope with leading a much larger team?

Do they know how to put in place all the essential health and safety practices or make sure others in the team are doing so? Can you trust that they will make sure every aspect of the event is covered by the relevant insurances and that they'll ensure the necessary legal due diligence is done?

These contextual matters are important to consider before anyone starts work. Your leader or producer will likely have to pick and choose the right creative or content solutions if there is a choice to be made that others on the team can't, or won't, make. They are ultimately in charge of all aspects of the event, responsible for getting it over the line in line with its objectives, and/or maintaining the integrity of its design, purpose and/or creative vision.

Key role 2: content lead. Next up is someone to lead the content side of things – the director in theatre terminology. This clearly needs to be someone with relevant content experience. Contextual experience, while a bonus, is not the key qualification here.

For an art, cultural or entertainment event, this role will almost certainly be an artist or group of artists, a designer or creative director. A musician on their concert tour would be the content lead. They may have musical directors, choreographers, set designers and others working with them and advising them, they may even have various assistants and managers if they are too busy themselves, but still the artist would likely be the ultimate lead. It is their art; their talent; their content or themselves on show. Similarly, an artist creating street or performance art would be the content lead for their performances, while a comedian would be the content lead for their comedy show.

A festival or cultural event bringing together all manner of art and entertainment needs a creative director, artistic director or similar. At a sports event, the content lead would typically be the sporting director, competition director, or whoever's responsible for ensuring the competition is fair and legal, the equipment and environment (the field of play) up to scratch, and the competitors are looked after. Job titles are irrelevant. The content lead may also be the CEO, managing director, producer, or have any other titles, roles and responsibilities. What is key

here is making sure they are qualified and suitable to be the content lead.

Sports events are a good example of an amalgamation of many small events, which I will cover in more detail later on. A sporting event may well have an opening ceremony, too. In this case, the event is simply split into smaller recognisable events with the core roles identified for each one. In the example of the sporting event, part of the event would see the content lead being the sporting or competition director, while the opening ceremony would have its own content lead, likely someone creative.

For a brand or marketing event or exhibition, the content lead may be the brand or product manager, or it may be a creative director from an agency if they have the required knowledge and insight. It may even be the chief executive of a smaller brand or organisation if they have the time. Remember, this isn't about job titles; it's about who's best qualified and able to be the content lead.

They may have a creative designer or an entire army of content creation people reporting to them, but the content lead takes responsibility for leading and proactively driving forward the content development and/or the creative integrity of the event. A government event, for example a large summit or conference, would likely see the content lead being the policy lead for the summit or the lead person from the department commissioning the live event. This person would need to have insight and knowledge of the subject matter: the content at the event. The content lead may be someone from a third party, like an event agency, if they have the necessary insight and authority, but this would be unusual for a government event, as most governments would want to sign off and approve everything. However, it is not unheard of, especially if a government department is already overworked.

Quite often, the content lead is seen as a creative role, but content shouldn't be confused with creative. If the event is about communication or sales, the content lead should be the person most qualified and empowered to lead the direction of the content, messaging and objectives. They may have creative people, like a creative director, reporting to them, but the content comes first.

The content lead understands and has the authority to ensure that the integrity of the content is upheld, making any necessary decisions accordingly. They are ultimately in charge of all aspects of the event's content.

Key role 3: technical and infrastructure lead. The third member of the team, or the third role, is someone to deliver all the physical and technical elements of the event. Whatever event you're planning will take place in or on something. There will be physical elements.

It's important this person has relevant contextual experience. Are they capable of dealing with budgets, scale, timescales, locations, venues, types of infrastructure, and any research and development or manufacturing necessary to the success of the event? For a simple event, for example a small conference, the technical and infrastructure lead may be the person responsible for planning and delivering the set and staging. The technical and infrastructure lead for an exhibition, experiential, arts or entertainment event is going to lead the management and supervision of technical, scenic, branding production and staging contractors (and construction requirements, if necessary) during the planning stages. They will then supervise all these roles during the event's delivery, making sure the content requirements are developed and delivered in line with the designs, scopes or specifications from the content teams. They will work proactively with the content lead and team should plans, designs or any other content need altering or modifying for operational, practical or technical reasons.

A sporting event will see the technical and infrastructure (the overlay) lead taking the lead on any construction or manufacturing requirements, be it scenery, branding, groundworks and landscaping, or constructing permanent or temporary venues. Their role would also include any shipping, freighting or transportation requirements. If it relates to the physical delivery of the event, it falls under this person's remit. They may have a raft of people supporting them, from technicians and site managers through to stage managers and wardrobe managers, but they all need leading and managing.

Typically called the technical director, production director, production manager, infrastructure manager, overlay manager or head of production to name but a few titles, this person is ultimately responsible for making sure the physical and technology requirements for the event are developed then delivered.

Key role 4: operations and logistics.
The final key role is someone to take care of the operations or logistics. Specifically, this role includes any venue or location research, organisation and scheduling of travel, accommodation, catering, hospitality, ticketing, welfare, accreditation, venue liaison, site and staffing operations, registration requirements and similar. As with the previous role, it's important this person has relevant contextual experience above all else. Experience of the event's content may help, but it isn't mandatory.

For example, I was once leading a large cultural festival involving hundreds of artists and performers from around the globe descending on a major city to perform on numerous occasions at different locations across the city for over a month. Given that this was an event dominated by theatre and arts with theatrical people in various senior management roles, there was some pressure on me to use someone with a theatre or arts background to look after the travel and accommodation requirements – a company manager or artist liaison manager, for example, who was primarily used to dealing with artists.

This logical assumption may well have worked, but the role meant leading and coordinating thousands of constantly changing flight and accommodation requirements. The additional issues this would throw up and the inevitable changes in plans that would arise from the artists' preferences or any changes in the festival's programme would only add to the pressure. Neither I nor the project had the time or money to take someone through a learning curve; I needed someone with demonstrable experience of dealing with these contextual issues. Whether they came from the arts world was, for this role, less important.

I engaged someone who was used to dealing with large-scale international corporate roadshows and summits;

events with thousands of people coming and going and continually changing their plans – identical contextual skills to the role this particular festival required.

Often referred to as the operations director/manager, logistics director/ manager, event planner/manager or similar, the person in this role assumes ultimate responsibility for all operational and logistics requirements for participants, performers, VIPs, guests, spectators, cast, crew, staff, or anyone else.

Responsibility for roles

These four key roles can all be undertaken by the same person or up to four different people. I've assumed them all for some smaller projects, or two or three of them for slightly larger events, but typically, I have assumed just one role. People in these roles can have committees reporting to them if necessary, or they may even report in to a committee or board themselves if the event is part of a larger initiative, but the roles should never be the responsibility of a committee or more than one person. Each role needs one person to be responsible, empowered and accountable.

There is a reason why the military has clear lines of communication and directly accountable individuals. The armed forces work in fast-moving environments and the situation they find themselves in can change rapidly, so their leaders need to make decisions immediately. Live events, as the event date approaches, are no different. You will be required to make decisions quickly, sometimes immediately, and these decisions

need to be made by a single person if you're to keep on track and on target as you charge towards your immovable deadline. You need to be able to look at any single part of your live event and know:

- Which **one** person is responsible for leading it
- Which **one** person is responsible for its content
- Which **one** person is responsible for its technical delivery
- Which **one** person is responsible for the logistics and operations

If you don't have a clear, unambiguous name for each of these roles, there will be unnecessary confusion and wasted time and money. Everyone involved in the event needs to have clear direction.

This is often a challenge as responsibility can seem scary, and some people run a mile from accountability. Some organisations may even frown upon a single individual making important and high-impact decisions alone. You need people who will take responsibility and who are empowered to do so, though. If someone isn't comfortable, able or empowered to make decisions whenever they're needed without consulting a committee, either they are the wrong person for the role, or the governance needs addressing to empower them. Of course, they may have committees, boards, groups, departments, or advisors they can consult, but at some point with most events, there will come a time when either they don't have the time to consult a committee, or they will have to make a decision without having all the necessary information or authority from elsewhere. This is why the people in the four key roles need to have relevant contextual and content experience. Their sixth sense helps.

No matter the size of the event, be it a small meeting or the Olympic Games, it should have this proven structure, these four key roles in place. Some events are multifaceted, so having just four roles and up to four people

covering them clearly isn't feasible. In more complex instances, the event is simply divided into distinguishable smaller events, each with its own four roles in place.

For example, a multi-sport event needs the four key roles clearly identified to look after each individual sport. A music festival with numerous areas, events or stages needs to be divided into individual elements with the core set of four roles in place for each element. Similarly, an exhibition, large conference or experiential marketing event with numerous areas, elements or sub-events needs to be split accordingly with sets of the four roles in place.

Of course, having multiple teams working on one event requires coordination. This is easily achieved if the project lead of each element reports to a project lead for the entire event, and all the content leads of each sub-event report to an overall content lead. The overall leader supports the lead of each individual element while giving them the autonomy to undertake their role. And just as one person may assume more than one role within a core team of four, one person may also undertake multiple roles across a larger structure, subject to their ability and the event requirements.

For example, if an event has a number of small elements, as detailed in Figure 2.3, one technical lead (marked 'A') may be able to lead the planning and development of all the technical requirements of each sub-event. One content lead (marked 'B') may be able to lead the development of the content across all or a number of different sub-events. The person who is taking on each role for each element of the event needs to be clear, though. Everyone needs to know who to turn to and who's leading each element.

Some people have many different talents. When an individual has more than one skill or area of expertise, separate them. I worked once with a great event director who also happened to know a lot about the content of the event, and in a former life had been a logistics manager, too. This person undertook multiple roles on one event, but each skill was separate. The work they did with regard to the content of the event fell under the creative director's supervision, and the logistics work they did fell under the remit and supervision of the event's logistics director.

Just because someone has many talents doesn't mean you alter the team structure to accommodate them; instead, you work out where each of their skills fits into the proven team structure.

Multi-Part Corporate Event

Executive   Creative
Producer   or Content
                 Director

Conference

Producer   Creative   Production   Logistics or
            or Content   Lead   Operations
            Director   Lead

Staff, crew, contractors

Gala Dinner

Producer   Creative   Production   Logistics or
            or Content   Lead   Operations
            Director   Lead

Staff, crew, contractors

Expo

Producer   Creative   Production   Logistics or
            or Content   Lead   Operations
            Director   Lead

Staff, crew, contractors

Figure 2.3: Multi-part event role duplicates

Other roles and figureheads

When I explain the four key roles structure to people, be they someone commissioning an event (a client), a client's in-house event team, or an event agency, organising committee or similar, they repeatedly bring up two concerns. The first issue is the question around who the public leader, the outwardly facing owner or figurehead of the event is. The second question involves numerous other roles that are typically assumed to be leadership roles yet are not mentioned in the core structure of four roles.

We'll look at each concern in turn.

Figurehead. Most events serve as an important PR tool for the organisers to aim at their audience. The person commissioning the event – the person right at the top of the food chain, if you like – can often want to be seen as the event's figurehead.

For example, the brand manager of a new product will, rightly, see the product launch as their event, and will likely be live on camera and in the media speaking about the new product. They will consider themselves the lead of the event. An artist having their art installed or performed in a public space will see themselves as the event's lead and spokesperson. After all, the content of the event is their art. The chairman or CEO of a large sporting event's organising committee will see themselves as the lead of the event, as will most of the host nation's population and media.

It is important, though, not to confuse the project lead – the person leading the core team of four roles – with the public face, public lead or figurehead of an event. They can be different people. The core team of four needs leading by someone with the relevant contextual experience. Unless the public face of an event has this skillset and the time to lead, direct or produce the event day to day, they can't assume the role of leading the core team responsible for delivering the event. Which is fine, the figurehead is merely the public face or spokesperson, while the core team, working closely with or advising the figurehead leads the event's development.

There is no reason at all why the public face of the event can't also perform one of the other roles in the core team. An artist, for example, may be the content lead of the event while almost certainly being its public face. Similarly, a brand manager may be both the content lead on the core team (if they have the time and inclination) and the event owner or the public face leading a product launch, but there will always need to be someone with the relevant contextual experience working with them, leading the project and the team behind the scenes.

Other roles. The second point people tend to raise when they're looking at the structure of four key roles is that there are numerous other roles they think should be part of the core team. Depending which sector they're in, these roles may include senior management personnel, account managers, procurement, marketing, sponsorship, finance, commercial and legal roles, designers, chief executives, human resources...I could list every senior or leadership role under the sun.

Yes, these roles may be important; essential, even. However, that doesn't alter the makeup of the core team of four roles you need to lead an event. All the other roles simply work with or report in to one or all of the four key roles. Which of the four key roles the additional personnel or senior management report to or work with isn't overly important and will vary event by event. You are producing an event, though, or having one produced, so the event's needs come first and must be led and directed by those with the relevant experience, just as an architect would lead the development of a new building or a producer and director would lead the production of a film. In my experience, though, this often leads to concerns and, on occasion, arguments, which often has more to do with individuals' egos than the needs of an event.

Let's consider an example. An account manager within an event agency may see themselves as the lead of an event. If they are also the producer, working on and leading the event day to day, they are indeed the lead of the core team of four roles. However, if they are an interface between the client and the agency, their role is a relationship role or, more accurately, a sales role. They are there to nurture and reassure the client and support the core team leading the event; they work with or report to the event's lead, or have the event's lead report to them on regular occasions. This is an important distinction which needs to be clear from the outset to avoid confusion, duplication of work and wasted time or money.

Sponsorship, marketing, public relations, design, digital and almost any other type of role are often key linchpins within an event team, and can make or break an event, but they are there to support the entire team where necessary. Who the people covering these roles report to within the core team of four principal roles is somewhat academic as they will be working with the whole team, or much of it. As long as they are positioned and empowered to support all the members of the core team, that's all that matters.

With all these additional roles, there needs to be a distinction between line-management and reporting lines, which are HR issues, and how various roles practically support everyone on the core team. If it's important for your own governance that the myriad of additional roles has a clear line manager within the core team, the choice of who the line manager is can be a somewhat arbitrary decision. Again, what's important is that they are positioned and empowered to support the entire team.

Any team needs to be structured in such a way that the people in the four key roles are clearly identifiable and accountable, but with as flat an architecture as possible. Everyone should be able to talk to everyone else, discuss anything openly and work together, but when decisions need making, they must know who's responsible for making them. Committees upon committees, while common in many organisations, are the death knell of producing events effectively and efficiently.

I have been asked to create and had to decipher too many team charts, organograms and personnel structures over the years. They are over-complicated, over-used, over-requested, and over the top in my view. I've never found them comprehensible or useful. Simply know who does what and who is accountable for what within in the team producing an event, and which of the core four roles each person reports to. Collaborative working with accountable individuals is the ideal. Make sure you either set this up or have it set up on your behalf.

You can visit the website www.TheFactsOfLive.com for more information about the differences between content and context and quick reference guides for the best way to structure teams to produce great events of all different types.

Summary

This chapter has provided an insight into the unique environment in which events are produced: constantly changing requirements, a fixed deadline, everyone watching, and rarely being in full control of everything affecting the event's success. We've outlined the important differences between content and context, then looked at the four key roles any event needs. This is an event's anatomy.

Whether you are planning on doing things yourself, building your own team or outsourcing, make sure you know, for every aspect of an event:

- Which **one** person is responsible for leading it (context experience is key)
- Which **one** person is responsible for its content (content experience is key)
- Which **one** person is responsible for its technical delivery (context experience is key)
- Which **one** person is responsible for the logistics and operations (context experience is key)

Each of these roles needs to be covered by an accountable, empowered and relevantly experienced individual. One person could do all or a few roles for a smaller event, but each role should never be covered by a committee or more than one person. Where a large event is actually a number of smaller events, a set of the four key roles needs to exist for each of the small events, the lead for each set reporting to a separate lead covering the entire event. Finally, the figurehead of an event can be anyone. It doesn't need to be the leader of the core team.

The roles alone aren't sufficient, though. The marriage of the roles coupled with the relevant content and context experience must be in place to make this work.

This structure is fundamental. If I ever get asked to look at, help sort out problems on or improve an event, more often than not, I can solve many issues by focusing on this team structure.

3

As in nature, the simpler a live event's structure, the more powerful the results.

Chapter 3

Live Event Team Structures

This chapter aims to address the most frequent questions about how best to structure teams of people to create and produce any type of live event, how to develop or harness ideas and innovation, how to deliver the most value, and, last but certainly not least, how to generate the biggest impact.

If you are putting a team together yourself, this chapter will serve as a guide. If you have someone else doing it for you, you'll gain a better understanding of what to ask for and what to expect.

I've described and discussed a number of different structures, to provide a rounded view of how the same principles can be applied and scaled across any live event.

How do you structure the best team?

More often than not, when groups of people come together to develop, conceive or produce an event, the people with the relevant experience are not involved at the right time. There are exceptions, of course, but time and time again I have seen so much time, money and effort being wasted on feasibility studies, consultancy work, forming committees, cost benefit analysis exercises and similar to determine how best to structure a team or group of people to produce live events.

When an event is a genuinely new idea, truly innovative or exceptionally complicated, there can be merit in feasibility or detailed research. Such events are the exception rather than the norm, though, and the structure of even the most complicated event can, and should, follow the principles in *The Facts Of Live*. My aim with this book is to provide a template: a level of clarity that can be used to support any event, giving you more confidence and helping you save your time and money. This in turn allows you and your team to get to the important content and contextual stuff that actually matters far more quickly. With the right structure in place, everyone involved has the support they need readily available and in a timely manner. Your event then has the best chance of creating the most impact for the best value with minimum risk.

For each of the structures we will look at in this chapter, I will provide indicative job titles to cover each of the four key roles. As we've discussed before, job titles are completely irrelevant, so the titles I've chosen are only for illustrative purposes. Please don't focus on the job titles of any of these roles; focus instead on what the people in each role should be doing. The job titles can be misleading if you take them literally.

While it would be fabulous if life were simple, few events fall neatly into just one of the categories we will look at in this chapter. Most have elements of a number of different types of event, so it's worth reading through all the examples to see how all events share more similarities than differences structurally and to gain greater clarity on how any event can be best structured. More examples and further support can be found at www.TheFactsOfLive.com

Street theatre structure

Let's look at a piece of street theatre or performance art in a public space. We need four key roles to lead such an event, as detailed in Figure 3.1.

The person in the role of producer leads all the activity. They make sure the money is in place to finance the event or they find the money, deal with any marketing, whether they do it themselves or outsource it, coordinate with any authorities and stakeholders, make sure insurance is in place and up to date to cover everyone and everything involved in the event, and help and support others in the team with whatever they need.

The creative director or artist leads the content and creative direction. They curate the art, artists, performers, or whatever else the artistic content may be.

The production lead oversees all and any infrastructure or physical requirements. This could include safety equipment in a public space, health and safety practices, any staging, technical or technology requirements, and making sure any costume and props requirements are taken care of. They may also need to undertake research and development or manufacturing for elaborate props or scenery.

The operations lead deals with all travel, accommodation, catering, hospitality and ticketing requirements if there are any, along with any other logistical or operational requirements for all artists and performers, staff, crew, public and spectators.

It's conceivable that all of these roles could be done by one person for a small piece of street theatre. For a larger piece of performance art in a public space, there could be hundreds of people reporting in to these four leads.

If the performance art is actually spread across numerous locations, it would be sensible to treat each area or performance as a separate sub-event. Identify who is responsible for

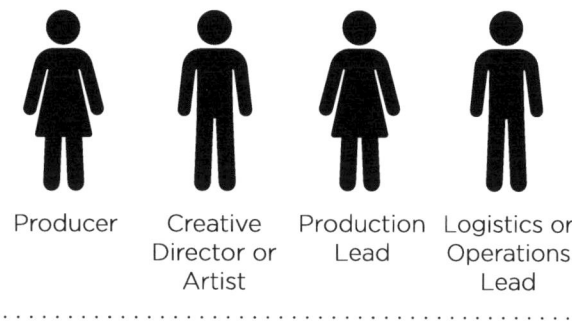

Street Theatre Core Roles

Producer   Creative Director or Artist   Production Lead   Logistics or Operations Lead

Staff, crew, volunteers, subcontractors

Figure 3.1: Street theatre single roles

each of the four key roles I've outlined above for each sub-event, and then simply have a lead producer and lead creative director or artist.

For example, if the performance is actually three sub-performances in different areas, the team would look like Figure 3.2.

There should be one (just one) accountable and authorised person clearly responsible for each role. Multiple roles may be undertaken by the same person if time and practicality allow. The people in any other roles and any subcontractors (vendors/suppliers) would report in to one of these four key roles.

Assuming the person taking on each role has the relevant content and/or contextual experience, they will be able to deal with any issues that arise in a timely manner and without fuss. There will therefore be no need for debate, committees or prolonged procrastination as work progresses. With this structure in place, the artist or creative director will be fully supported and can focus their efforts where they matter: producing great art or entertainment. Everyone else within the team will also be fully supported, and anyone outside the team will know exactly where to turn for the support or information they need, too.

Multiple Location Street Theatre Lead Roles

Executive
Producer

Creative
Director or
Artist

Street Theatre Location 1 Core Roles

Producer

Creative
Director or
Artist

Technical
Lead

Logistics or
Operations
Lead

. . . .

Staff, crew, volunteers, contractors

Street Theatre Location 2 Core Roles

Producer

Creative
Director or
Artist

Technical
Lead

Logistics or
Operations
Lead

. . . .

Staff, crew, volunteers, contractors

Street Theatre Location 3 Core Roles

Producer

Creative
Director or
Artist

Technical
Lead

Logistics or
Operations
Lead

. . . .

Staff, crew, volunteers, contractors

Figure 3.2: Multiple location street theatre roles

Launch, conference or experiential event structure

If you have a brand and you're intending to stage an event to launch a new product or service, or you're looking for a brand experience event, once again, four roles are key. This applies whether you're pulling your own team together or outsourcing the event through an event agency, production company or similar, or you could even combine in-house and external people to take on the four roles.

The four key roles for this type of event are shown in Figure 3.3.

The producer will be the person responsible for leading the event's development and, ultimately, its delivery. Their role will be to agree the requirements and brief along with the purpose of the product launch, and what criteria are to be met or measured (if any), be they specific tangible metrics or more artistic or subjective criteria.

They will then drive development forward, leading all involved in the event to ensure it is designed along whatever brief and criteria have been agreed or that materialise as time passes. They will lead the client, or if they are in house, the business or organisation they're working within, along with the whole team producing the event: the creative or content director, production, operations lead, and everyone else involved.

The buck stops with the producer; responsibility ultimately falls to them. They therefore need the relevant contextual experience and authority to drive the event forward, and sometimes make decisions without being in full possession of all the information they may want or need, making a sixth sense necessary. You have a product launch to deliver on time, in front of the world, live, so you will demand strong leadership from your producer. The producer should also be able to distinguish (and choose) good ideas from bad and good (or appropriate) creativity from poor creativity. While they are not the content or creative director, they are responsible for ensuring the event is fit for purpose or has creative integrity.

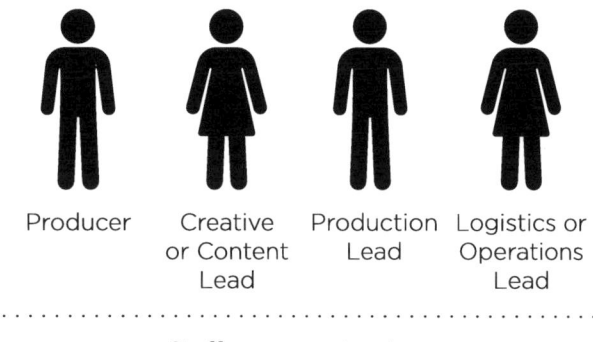

Product Launch / Experiential Event Core Roles

Producer Creative or Content Lead Production Lead Logistics or Operations Lead

Staff, crew, contractors

Figure 3.3: Product launch/experiential event core roles

The creative or content lead is the person who will take the lead on the event's purpose, its content, from the insights, strategy or research through to its creative direction. Logically, the best person for this would be a product or brand manager for the product you're intending to launch. Practically, however, it's unlikely such a person will have the time to get involved in the day-to-day detail of producing an event. If you have someone in the brand team or elsewhere in the organisation who can take the role on, that may work, if they have the time. Alternatively, a creative or content director, either in house, brought in on contract, or from an agency, can and often does work well.

It's important to differentiate between 'content' and 'creative'. The role here is about leading the content, which can often be a creative role, as most product launches are inherently the creative presentation of a product or service. If the person leading the content side of things is familiar with the content but is not creative,

they will need the relevant creative resources – a creative director or similar – reporting to and supporting them. If the person taking on this role is primarily a creative person, they will need to have the relevant knowledge about the content, the product or brand, or access to it.

As with all live event team structures, the production lead oversees all and any infrastructure or physical requirements. They will start by working with the creative and operations team to develop the design of the product launch. This could involve research and development into various technologies, planning how to stage the launch in suitable venues or locations, and supporting all involved to develop a tangible event. They will take care of any staging, technical or technology, manufacturing, infrastructure, scenic, props, costumes, stage management or similar requirements.

The operations lead deals with all and any travel, accommodation, catering, hospitality and other logistical or operations requirements for all those involved, for example presenters, staff, crew and the audience.

Other people required for a successful brand or corporate event include marketing, PR, media, health and safety, and procurement, along with any subcontractors (vendors). All of these people would report in to one of the four key roles (or people on these four roles' teams).

If your product launch is likely to be a more complex event with activity in different places, perhaps different venues or cities, or with a number of sub-events taking place, perhaps a conference, exhibition and dinner as different elements of a large overall event, simply break down the event into its component parts and assign the four keys roles to each part. And then, each set of four roles will report in to an overall producer and overall content or creative lead.

Figure 3.4 illustrates this.

As always, some roles, if it's practical, could be undertaken by the same person. It is key, though, to make sure that everyone can easily identify the one person who is responsible for each role. You then have on tap, assuming you have ensured that each person taking on each of the key roles has the relevant content and/or contextual experience, all the expertise and advice you need to make sure your event is a success.

It is worth noting that if you are using an external organisation, production company or agency, you may have a great many other roles suggested or offered to you. You may even request them yourself. Roles such as accounts, sales, or HR have more to do with selling, relationships, communication and redundancy (backup or contingency) than they do with the event specifically, and should therefore be judged on their own merit. It is the four key roles that are key to developing and producing the product launch you need. Establish those first and then consider further roles on a case-by-case basis.

If you're running an agency or production company, you may want or need an account management structure or similar in addition to the core team of four key roles. If this is the case, make sure that you separate the roles clearly. The four key roles are what you (and in turn, your clients) need to develop, produce and deliver a great event. An account management team or structure has more to do with sales, client retention and business development. If the line between these roles becomes blurred, it causes confusion and helps neither you nor your clients. It certainly won't help the event, so

ensure there's clarity between the roles from the outset. Again, some people may undertake more than one role. They could be both the account manager and the producer, but these are separate roles and need identifying as such.

This structure, the four key roles, leads to everyone being squarely focused on the event and creating the most impact possible. This approach will inherently deliver the best value as you will have a talented, streamlined, straightforward team with relevant experience and clear leadership. By having the right and relevant experience in the right place at the right time, you will greatly reduce risks, too.

Product Launch / Experiential Event Lead Roles

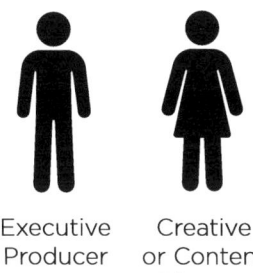

Executive
Producer

Creative
or Content
Director

Conference Core Roles

Producer

Creative
or Content
Director

Production
Lead

Logistics or
Operations
Lead

Staff, crew, contractors

Exhibition Core Roles

Producer

Creative
or Content
Director

Production
Lead

Logistics or
Operations
Lead

Staff, crew, contractors

Gala Dinner Core Roles

Producer

Creative
or Content
Director

Production
Lead

Logistics or
Operations
Lead

Staff, crew, contractors

Figure 3.4: Product launch/experiential event lead roles

Sports event structure

Sports events come in many flavours. Regardless of the sport or the type of sporting event, be it professional, amateur or mass participation, it needs to be led by a core team of four.

Figure 3.5 shows the core team in the context of a sports event.

The event director is responsible for driving the event forward, shaping it, its funding, marketing and commercial aspects, whether they take on these tasks themselves, have others involved internally, or outsource them. Much of their time will likely be taken up supporting the stakeholders involved, who in turn will guide and support the rest of the team.

The sport or competition director takes the lead on, unsurprisingly, all elements of the sport or competition. They look after the participants and oversee the rules and regulations, either creating them or ensuring everyone adheres to the existing rules. They make sure that the arena, the area the sport happens in or the field of play is designed in line with the sport's requirements or guidelines. They lead on how the sport is presented to the spectators or audience, both as a visual spectacle and via any technology or entertainment to enhance spectators' experiences. In addition, they oversee all the resources that may be required to facilitate or support the sport, be that medical provision, compliance, prize money or similar. If it relates to the sporting activity itself, it lies within the sport or competition director's remit.

The technical lead heads up all the infrastructure and fit-out (or 'overlay' as it's often referred to in sporting circles), technical and technology requirements. This could be anything from having a new venue built (clearly they wouldn't do this themselves, but they would oversee the people who are doing so) to preparing an existing venue or public space. Their role will include all infrastructure, any manufacturing required, and the design or provision of all technology,

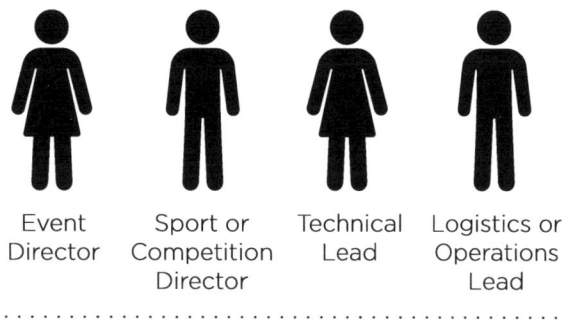

Sports Event Core Roles

Event Director   Sport or Competition Director   Technical Lead   Logistics or Operations Lead

Staff, crew, volunteers, contractors

Figure 3.5: Sports event core roles

both general event technology and sport-specific technology such as timing equipment. The requirements for the event specifically and the preparation of the venue can sometimes be seen as different roles or dealt with in silos. The technical lead should oversee and coordinate them both, though – themselves or with their team.

The operations or logistics lead heads up all travel, accommodation, accreditation, catering, hospitality and any other logistical or operations requirements for all those involved, be they athletes, participants, volunteers, staff, crew or spectators.

All other roles and resources report in to one of these core roles where relevant. The external resources and subcontractors – the 'functional areas' as such services and provisions are often referred to in the sports sector – are there to serve the needs of the event and those leading it, so they too report in to the relevant part of the core team.

For example, if a sports event is being broadcast on television, there will be a TV production team. This team needs to report in to one of the four key roles (or to someone within one of the four key roles' respective teams). It doesn't really matter whom they report in to, as long as it's one of these roles, although it may make sense for the producer and director of the TV broadcast to report in to the sporting or competition director, the TV technical production team to report in to the technical lead, and the TV production team's coordinator to report in to the operations lead. Whatever works for you or your team is fine, as long as everyone reports in to a key role in some way, shape or form.

Similarly, if the sporting event needs branding designing and producing, it will likely need a design team or creative director overseeing this. This person or team could report in to the event director or the sporting or competition director – it really doesn't matter, as long as it's clear whom they report to and who's responsible for supporting and overseeing them. The production and delivery of the branding would likely fall under the technical lead's remit and supervision. If the branding design and production are being provided by one external company, again, this is fine. The design side of the operation will report to the event director or sport or competition director (or someone beneath them), and the delivery side will liaise with and be supervised by the technical lead.

If the sports event has a raft of sports presentation initiatives, such as audiovisual and theatrical mechanisms to bring the sporting action and results to life, ensure that the person or organisation leading on this reports in to one of the four key roles, be it the event director, the sport or competition director, or someone in their respective teams.

Many sporting events quickly find themselves becoming unnecessarily complex. This is usually due to the number of organisations involved. For professional sporting events, these organisations can include national and international sporting federations, regional sports groups, venues, governments, local authorities, and many more. What starts out as a fairly straightforward requirement, the facilitation of sporting activity, can rapidly escalate, costing more, taking longer to develop and deliver, and causing more confusion and concern than it needs to.

These complexities can be avoided, or at least greatly reduced, if the core team is established from the outset. This core team, if they've got the right content and contextual experience, and if they have the authority, will provide strong leadership that drives the project forward, ensuring everyone involved focuses on what's important and shielding them from noise or unnecessary distraction. This strong leadership also drastically reduces wasted time and money as everyone involved will have clearly identified individuals to take the lead, be accountable and direct all activity. And the right team in the right place at the right time will identify and plan for any risks long before they are ever likely to manifest.

Multi-sport events structure

Multi-sport events are similar to single sport events, apart from the fact that they, clearly, consist of more than one sport. Many different sports may happen in the same place, for example various athletics disciplines in a stadium, or across numerous different venues, like an Olympic, Paralympic or Commonwealth Games.

The core structure for each sport and area/venue can remain the same, with four key roles for each sub-event reporting in to overall leads. In addition, it is highly likely there will be ancillary sub-events in and around the sporting action. These may include ceremonies, sponsors' activations and entertainment.

Figure 3.6 illustrates an example of this structure.

I have detailed the responsibilities of each of the roles in the previous sections. In short, the project manager for each sport drives that event's planning and delivery forward. The sport or competition director leads on all sporting rules, regulations, and similar requirements. The technical or production lead is responsible for anything relating to the venue or construction of venues, technology and infrastructure, and similar. The operations lead heads up all travel, accommodation, catering, hospitality and any other logistical or operations requirements for all those involved. It is again conceivable, if it's practical, that more than one of these roles can be taken on by one person. It's essential, though, to identify who is responsible for each role, even if the same name appears in different places.

Similarly, any ceremonies or ancillary events will have a lead, someone responsible for the creative or content elements, and someone responsible for the physical and operational elements. Any other staff, subcontractors or functional areas are there to serve the event or provide the functions of the event, and therefore report in to the relevant lead of each event.

Given the scale, perceived complexity and politics involved in multi-sports events, it is tempting, and common, for organisers to create huge committees and boards to work out how best to plan and develop the event. There are many factors to consider and plan for, from funding and sponsorship through to construction work and new infrastructure, but work needs to start with the requirements of the events and the core teams leading the events and sub-events. If the person taking on each key role has the right content and/or contextual experience, they will dictate, lead and guide all the other requirements. If the four key roles are brought in at a later date, after committees, consultants, functional area leads and infrastructure professionals have been deliberating on the best approach and solutions, the likelihood is that the people covering the key roles will at best struggle to rationalise, and at worst be hindered by decisions, structures and processes made by people who don't have the necessary content or contextual experience.

I have been asked to look at, plan and support numerous events of this nature, often needing to solve or foresee problems that may arise during their planning and development. Almost without exception, any issues and problems that arise come down to the fact that when I ask which one person is leading a certain element, for example, which one person is responsible for the content, sport or competitive elements, or which one person is responsible for the physical elements, I rarely get an answer. I spend most of my time unpicking complex corporate structures and committees, eventually finding out that no one person is accountable or responsible for any of the core roles. As a result, moving anything forward efficiently is almost impossible.

I understand why this happens. Multi-sport events are typically extremely high profile with national and sporting reputations on the line. As a result, either consciously or subconsciously, the organisers

Multi-Sport Event Lead Roles

Event
Director

Director
of Sports

Athletics Events Core Roles

Project
Manager

Sport or
Competition
Director

Technical
Lead

Logistics or
Operations
Lead

Staff, crew, volunteers, functional areas, contractors

Swimming Events Core Roles

Project
Manager

Sport or
Competition
Director

Technical
Lead

Logistics or
Operations
Lead

Staff, crew, volunteers, functional areas, contractors

Cycling Events Core Roles

Project
Manager

Sport or
Competition
Director

Technical
Lead

Logistics or
Operations
Lead

Staff, crew, volunteers, functional areas, contractors

Ceremonies Core Roles

Producer

Creative
Director

Production
Lead

Logistics or
Operations
Lead

Staff, crew, volunteers, functional areas, contractors

Figure 3.6: Multi-sport event team structure

tend to adopt a safety-in-numbers philosophy. They hire more and more people without first getting the core roles established, and as a result, the event becomes increasingly difficult to manage and drive forward. Yet these difficulties could be avoided entirely by having the four key roles in place from the outset.

If you have the luxury of being able to hire as many people as you like, or indeed if you believe it to be necessary for any number of governance reasons, this is absolutely no problem. First, though, ensure you have the core roles in place. Ensure the people covering them have the correct content and contextual experience, and ensure they are empowered with the authority to make the decisions they will need to make. Then, and only then, when you have the relevant and appropriate expertise on tap, should you start looking at all the other roles you may need, making sure everyone reports in to one of the key roles.

Concert structure

We're looking at a music concert this time, but yet again, the four key roles are relevant, as detailed in Figure 3.7.

A concert will almost always be focused around the artist or musician's content: their music and performance. They will be the content lead. They may well have assistants to help them do this, given many musicians have busy schedules, but the artist on stage is inherently the content (or creative) lead.

If the concert consists of a number of acts or artists – a tribute concert, for example – then the creative director will need to be the person programming the concert. This may well be the same person who's taking on the role of producer or similar, or it could be someone whose role is to focus only on the artists, acts and performers on stage. Either way, one person needs clear creative and curatorial control to lead and direct the concert's content; in other words, who gets booked to perform.

The producer will lead the development of the concert, working hand in hand with the artists or content lead to drive the event forward. They will oversee all commercial, sponsorship, marketing, promotion, production and stakeholder relations and requirements. They are there to lead and support everyone else with whatever they need and whatever the concert needs.

In the public eye, the artist or artists will likely, rightly and understandably, be seen as the lead as it's their concert. However, behind the scenes, the producer pulls together all aspects of the concert and drives it forward. The producer may well be the artist if they are just starting out or have a passion for producing their own shows or events. It's important, though, that the two roles are clearly identified as separate roles, even if they are undertaken by the same person.

The production lead oversees all physical, technical and venue requirements. This could be anything to do with venue construction and modification, staging, scenery, technology, safety requirements, stage management, or props and scenery.

The operations or logistics lead will lead on all travel, accommodation, catering, hospitality, ticketing if there is any, and any other logistical or operational requirements for all artists and performers, staff, crew, public and spectators.

Again, there may be numerous other people on the team, but everyone should report in to one of these four roles. All subcontractors and other third parties will report in to members of this core team, too.

Clearly defined roles, clear areas of responsibility, and a fully supported and tightknit team will, if everyone has the relevant content and contextual experience, ensure all efforts are focused on creating a concert with the most impact for the best value, and mitigating or limiting any risks.

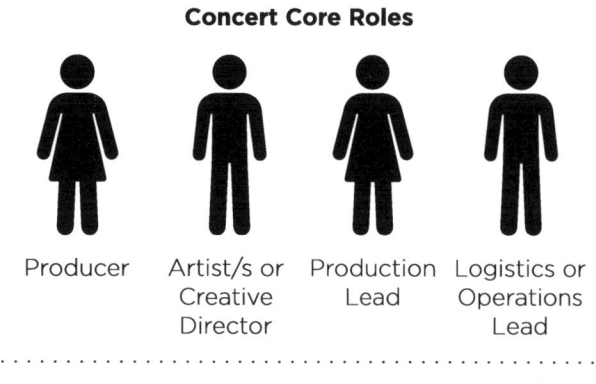

Concert Core Roles

Producer | Artist/s or Creative Director | Production Lead | Logistics or Operations Lead

Staff, crew, contractors

Figure 3.7: Concert core roles

Festival structure

While similar to the concert structure we have just looked at, a festival's structure will typically see a number of concerts and other activities happening concurrently. If a festival has three concert stages and a glamping area ('glamping' is glamorous or luxury camping), the structure will be as illustrated in Figure 3.8.

Each of the festival's music stages will have its own team, as will the glamping area. It may be possible for some of the lead roles to be carried out by the same person, though this needs assessing on a case-by-case basis and may change as the festival's plans evolve, which is both common and absolutely fine. What is important, though, is clearly identifying who is taking on each role at any given time, even if some roles are being undertaken by the same person.

Just as with the concert example, each stage at a festival needs a producer, or someone leading its planning and development. They will support and be supported by the artist, creative director or content lead for each stage: the person who is responsible for the talent and/or performances on stage. Each stage will then have a production lead overseeing and driving forward all technical, staging, scenic, venue, health and safety, stage management, and similar requirements, with the operations lead leading on the travel, accommodation, catering, hospitality, ticketing if there is any, and any other logistical or operations requirements for all artists and performers, staff, crew, public and spectators.

The glamping site will have a project manager or similar: someone to drive the planning and development of the area forward within the overall festival. They will coordinate all activity, oversee any marketing, commercial and regulatory requirements, including all the necessary insurance, and support the rest of the team.

The content lead will oversee the design of the glamping area, for example the types of tents and their

Festival Lead Roles

Festival or Event Director

Creative or Content Director

Stage 1 Core Roles

Producer

Artist/s or Creative Director

Production Lead

Logistics or Operations Lead

Staff, crew, contractors

Stage 2 Core Roles

Producer

Artist/s or Creative Director

Production Lead

Logistics or Operations Lead

Staff, crew, contractors

Stage 3 Core Roles

Producer

Artist/s or Creative Director

Production Lead

Logistics or Operations Lead

Staff, crew, contractors

Glamping Area Core Roles

Project Manager

Content Lead or Designer

Production Lead

Logistics or Operations Lead

Staff, crew, contractors

Figure 3.8: Festival team structure

fit-out, developing additional content in this space, such as entertainment or activities for the glampers. The content lead may be the same person as the producer if that's practical, but as always, it needs to be clear to everyone who the person undertaking this role is.

The production lead will oversee all physical requirements: venue and venue preparation, health and safety, manufacture or hire of the facilities required, technology and infrastructure, and staffing. The operations lead, as always, will lead on the travel, accommodation, ticketing or booking requirements, catering, hospitality and similar. In other words, these two key roles cover all the elements that affect the staff, crew, participants and guests at the glamping site. Again, all subcontractors and other third parties will report in to the relevant members of the core teams.

The lead of each of the elements of a festival will report in to an overall producer/festival director/event director (or similar). The various content leads report in to the festival's overall content lead or creative director, or similar.

There is clear logic in combining some roles, or the activities undertaken by some roles. For example, it makes sense to look at much of the work the operations leads take on regarding travel and accommodation for the whole festival rather than dealing with it individually stage by stage. Similarly, the festival's overall creative director or content lead may take on the same role for one of the festival's stages. As always, though, you need to be crystal clear on who is taking on each role, even if some people are taking on more than one role. Without this, you end up with a lack of accountability, creating more confusion than is necessary. Clear roles, occupied by people with relevant and proven content and contextual experience, result in an entire team or operation focusing on what's most important rather than solving needless problems.

Tradeshow, exhibition or expo structure

A tradeshow, exhibition or expo is usually an event that sees a site, venue or location prepared and made available for exhibitors to build or install their own stand, event, exhibit, pavilion or experience. Collectively, these individual exhibitors provide content relative to a specific industry, trade, issue or purpose. The tradeshow or exhibition is again best served by four key roles, as illustrated in Figure 3.9.

The exhibition director takes on the full responsibility for the exhibition. It is their job to guide the venture or business forward. They will also oversee the whole team and lead on sales, sponsorship, marketing and stakeholder engagement – whether they do it themselves or have entire teams or external organisations supporting them to do so.

The content lead is responsible for the tone, theme, messaging and creative direction of the exhibition, along with any strategy, insight or research work required. They will lead, find or work with the exhibitors and those participating at or contributing to the overall purpose of the exhibition, setting the framework around which the exhibition will be developed and providing guidance to the exhibitors and all involved. While working with the rest of the team, they will lead the curation and oversee exhibitors' plans and proposals.

The production lead will lead on all technical and infrastructure requirements. They will set the physical parameters the exhibitors or those participating need to work within, providing guidance on what technical facilities exist and what exhibitors need to provide themselves. They will also oversee the provision of all the technical and infrastructure requirements of the elements the exhibition organiser is undertaking themselves.

On larger tradeshows or expos, the production lead may need to oversee the construction of new buildings, refurbishments, or new technical infrastructure. Clearly such work will demand enormous teams, maybe even numerous companies, yet the production lead needs to take overall responsibility for all activity.

The operations lead will lead on the travel, accommodation, catering, hospitality, and any ticketing or booking requirements the exhibition organiser has, providing guidance or support to the operational and logistical needs of the individual exhibitors.

Each of the individual exhibitors needs their own team of people leading their overall direction, content, production and operational requirements. If the exhibition organiser intends to be an exhibitor too, their exhibition stand needs to have its own core team identified.

The exhibition organisers may need to report in to a board or a larger organisation, and may have various figureheads appearing to lead the tradeshow, exhibition or expo publicly. However, as always, the core four

roles need to be clearly identified and covered by someone with the relevant experience as, behind the scenes, it is they who will be producing and developing the event.

As with the examples we've covered so far, if the exhibition is in fact a number of exhibitions in different locations, venues, parts of a large venue, or even in different cities at the same time, each distinct area must have its own lead team of four core roles reporting in to an overall exhibition director and content lead. Where it's practical, some of these roles can be adopted by the same people or each can be covered by different people (but never more than one person). Either way, each role needs a clearly identifiable person with relevant content and contextual experience.

With all the core teams in place, eliminating or at least foreseeing and mitigating risks, the exhibition organisers can focus on what matters: driving sales and increasing the presence and impact of the exhibition.

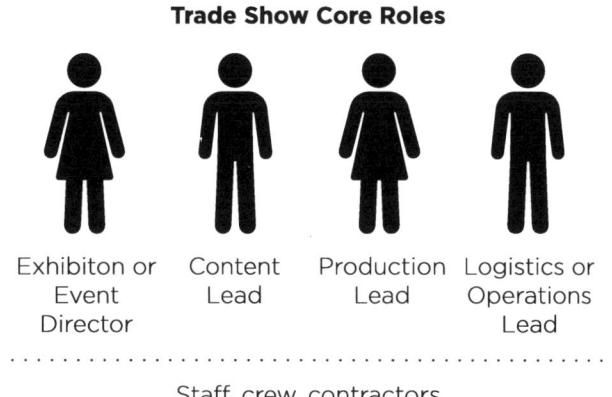

Trade Show Core Roles

Exhibiton or Event Director | Content Lead | Production Lead | Logistics or Operations Lead

Staff, crew, contractors

Figure 3.9: Trade show or expo core roles

Exhibition stand, expo or sponsor pavilion structure

Exhibitions, expos and pavilions (semi-permanent venues or buildings) can often be considered buildings or architecture first, and live events second. As a result, such projects often start with people and teams from the retail, fit-out or construction industries. This can be misguided as the focus will primarily be on the practical elements of such a venture, with this resulting in content or creative elements that aren't as powerful as they might otherwise be. You're ultimately creating entertainment or a show. Start with the four key roles, just as with any other live event, and then bring in the fit-out, retail, architectural or construction expertise at the right time: that way you'll have the right balance of practical (context) and creative or content experience.

Start with a core team of four people, as illustrated in Figure 3.10.

The project director or manager, or whatever you want to call this role, will lead all activity. They'll liaise with any clients, stakeholders and the exhibition organisers to clarify all requirements, refine any briefs and guide the rest of the team forward. They will then brief, direct and manage the team.

The creative director will lead on the exhibition stand or pavilion's purpose, look, design and operation or flow: the visitors' experience. The content will be a mix of design and messaging, so there may well need to be a raft of different people involved. These people may include architects, artists and digital specialists for larger ventures. Smaller ventures may be possible with just one person creating everything, from the 3D design of the environment to any digital content on screen. No matter the scale, though, the creative side of things and the content need leadership: someone to guide the design and experience forward, briefing and supporting all those involved beneath them, picking and choosing what does work and discarding what doesn't, and providing clear creative and content direction from the outset. With

Exhibition Stand or Pavilion Core Roles

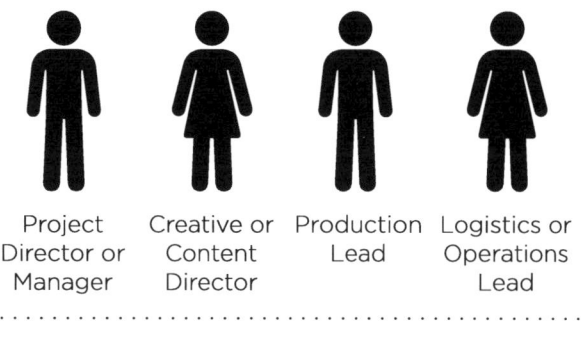

Project Director or Manager   Creative or Content Director   Production Lead   Logistics or Operations Lead

Staff, crew, contractors

Figure 3.10: Exhibition stand or pavilion core roles

strong singular creative leadership and direction, the design, impact and effectiveness of any exhibition or pavilion will be considerably more powerful, as it will not have been watered down by committees or conflicting ideas and design theories.

The production lead will lead on all physical elements, including any research and development, manufacturing, construction or engineering, installation, technical and technology requirements, health and safety oversight, stage management if relevant, scenic elements, props, and anything similar. They'll work hand in hand with the rest of the team during the initial design phases right through to delivery. They'll play a key role in liaising with the exhibition or event organisers to ensure everyone adheres to any venue requirements and requests all relevant facilities. They'll also ensure the exhibition stand or pavilion adheres to any guidelines set out by the event producers or exhibition organisers.

The operations lead is responsible for all travel, accommodation, catering, hospitality and any other logistical or operational requirements for everyone involved: VIPs, talent, staff, crew, and the audience. This may involve working closely with the exhibition organisers, making sure that all operational elements dovetail seamlessly with the overall event or exhibition's activities, and/or sharing or combining resources and plans where this is sensible.

Again, all subcontractors, staff and any other third parties will report in to this core team. And if the exhibition stand or pavilion has numerous sub-areas or sub-events, the four key roles need identifying for each area, with each core team reporting in to an overall project lead and content or creative lead.

If you are working with agencies, event companies, and production companies or similar, ensure there is clarity between their account, sales or relationship roles and the four key roles we have outlined. The account, sales and relationship roles may well be valuable additions to the team or a wider remit, but producing and developing the exhibition needs leading by the four key roles.

The four key roles are so important because, aside from this having been proven to be about as efficient a team structure as it's possible to have, all and any activities or issues sit neatly within one of the roles. There's no ambiguity or room for confusion, which means everyone can focus on what matters rather than sorting out issues that are often the result of an inappropriate team structure or members of the team not having the relevant content or contextual experience.

Political demonstration or rally structure

The rallies and demonstrations I am discussing here are the lawful and well-organised type. Such events are common, and when they're produced appropriately, everyone can focus on the issue that the demonstration or rally aims to address rather than organisational, safety or other failings. All those involved can direct as much effort as possible to making their points of view heard.

The four key roles needed for a rally or demonstration are illustrated in Figure 3.11.

The project or event director leads all activity. This person's role is to make sure the demonstration is financed, insured, coordinated, and delivered safely and legally. They are responsible for overseeing all marketing, communication, sponsorship (if relevant) and stakeholders, whether they do it themselves or have others supporting them.

The content lead is responsible for ensuring the message of the demonstration is clear, communicating that message to those likely to join the demonstration or rally, and leading on the content development of any ancillary activities like side events, conferences, entertainment or similar.

While it needs to be clear who's doing each of these roles, it is extremely common for both to be taken on by the same person. This is typically because the sheer determination and passion people require even to attempt, let alone pull off a demonstration or rally are considerable, and there is usually one person in any organisation or group who's the most passionate or driven.

For a smaller rally, it is certainly possible that one person could take on both these roles, but if you're looking at thousands of people attending a high-profile demonstration or rally in a metropolitan area, having one person attempt both roles would be short sighted.

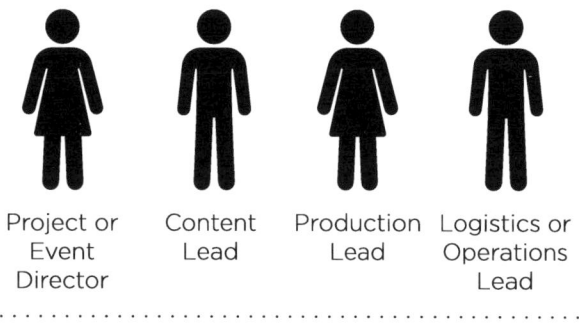

Political Demonstration Core Roles

Project or Event Director | Content Lead | Production Lead | Logistics or Operations Lead

Staff, crew, volunteers, contractors

Figure 3.11: Political demonstration core roles

The most driven and passionate individual in your team would almost certainly be the content lead and the public face of the movement or demonstration, calling people to action and providing the overall direction to messaging and content. Someone with relevant contextual experience would then be the project or event director. They'd be responsible for driving everything forward and making sure work progresses as it should, leaving the content lead free to rally support and promote the messages. The two roles are inherently different. One is about coordination, money, permissions and practicalities; the other is about garnering support. Muddling the two rarely works in my experience; passion and practicality are two different requirements. Passion can ride roughshod over practical necessities, while practicality can water down passion, drive and determination. You need a balance of each, which is why it's often best to have two separate people in these two key roles.

The production lead will then be responsible for all infrastructure, technology, security, stewarding, safety, staffing and similar. They will work with the relevant authorities, landowners and similar to discuss, plan and agree all physical requirements. Meanwhile, the operations lead will lead on all travel, accommodation, catering, hospitality and any ticketing or booking requirements for the team planning and delivering the rally. They will likely also lead on developing instructions and plans for travel, accommodation and welfare requirements for those attending with all relevant authorities and agencies (eg public transport organisations), then distributing that information publicly.

If the demonstration is to be in numerous locations, be they areas of one city or across many cities or countries, again, the event is simply split down into manageable sub-events. Each sub-event then has the four key roles reporting in to an overall project director and content lead.

Major public event structure

I've added this category as a catch-all for a number of types of events that don't really fit into any specific category, other than the fact they happen in public spaces and are typically outdoors. Events such as publicity stunts, ceremonies, firework displays and parades, for example.

As with every other type of event, public events need four key roles, as illustrated in Figure 3.12.

The producer will lead the entire operation. They will refine and develop the brief, requirements, measures of success and any other criteria with whomever the event is for. They will then convert this into a tangible brief and direction for the rest of the team.

The producer's role will then be to drive all activity forward. They'll lead and support the internal team. They will also lead and support any external stakeholders and third parties, for example emergency services, government organisations, venue owners or landowners, and any other people or organisations needed to help produce and develop a major public event. They will oversee all commercial and contractual arrangements, whether they manage them directly or have a team of commercial, legal, procurement or similar staff supporting them. They will also oversee or support all marketing, communication, sponsorship or PR requirements.

For a major public event (as is the case with many events), the marketing and communication activity can be inextricably linked to the success of the event. Too little marketing and the attendance or impact will be diminished. Too much marketing and the event may be unsafe if too many people turn up, also causing reputational issues. It's a balancing act for all parties involved.

The creative or content director will lead on the event's purpose. If it's a parade, for example, they will lead on the designs, music, choreography, staging and similar, in line with their own or their client's brief or direction. If it's a firework display, they will lead on and work with the pyrotechnic teams (or they may be a pyrotechnic designer if the event is purely a fireworks display), music, lighting and audio teams, and anyone else involved to craft a show or display in line with their or their client's vision.

If the public event is a publicity stunt, it will be similar to the product launch example we discussed previously. The content or creative director will be responsible for leading the design and development of the publicity stunt in a way that gets the right message across or presents the product or service in the most dramatic or powerful way possible. If they are more content focused than creative, they will need a creative person supporting them. If they are more creative than content focused, they will either need intimate knowledge of the product or service, or have someone on hand who has this knowledge.

As with the other examples, the production lead will drive forward all and any research and development, venue or location planning and liaison, authority liaison and permissions, technology, technical infrastructure, staging, scenic, props, stage management, and health and safety requirements. The operations lead leads on travel, accommodation, catering, hospitality, and any other logistical or operations requirements for all those involved. Depending on the event, they may need to look at the welfare and needs of the public, too, if there are requirements above and beyond what would otherwise be necessary in a public space.

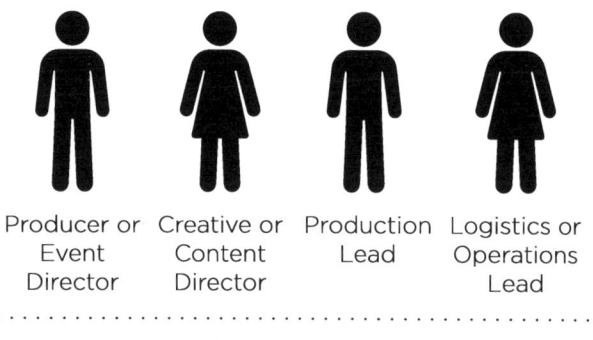

Public Event or PR Stunt Core Roles

Producer or Event Director | Creative or Content Director | Production Lead | Logistics or Operations Lead

Staff, crew, contractors

Figure 3.12: Public event or PR stunt core roles

All other staff, subcontractors and third parties report in to these four key roles, or those working with them.

If the major public event has many smaller events within it, or if it's spread out across different locations, cities or countries, each manageable sub-event needs to have four key roles clearly identified and reporting in to an overall producer or event director and overall content or creative director. Again, the public face of the event can be anyone; they don't necessarily need to be someone covering one of the four key roles.

There are many more examples of core team structures over at www.TheFactsOfLive.com

Summary

Any event or sub-event needs to have four core roles clearly defined and covered by people with the relevant content and/or contextual experience. Everyone involved in the creation and delivery of the event needs to have clarity on:

- Which **one** person is responsible for leading the event or sub-event (context experience is key)
- Which **one** person is responsible for its content (content experience is key)
- Which **one** person is responsible for its technical delivery (context experience is key)
- Which **one** person is responsible for the logistics and operations (context experience is key)

The four core roles don't need to be covered by people within the same organisation. If your organisation is producing its own event, you may have some of the roles covered in house, or contract someone in to fill one or more of them. If you're in a client–agency relationship, some roles may be covered by the agency, while others, such as the content lead, could be someone from the client organisation. If you have an event involving multiple stakeholders or organisations coming together to produce it, you may end up with four people from different organisations working together. This arrangement can work, but it is not without risk. You need to ensure that everyone clearly understands, and ideally states this understanding in writing, that the event's lead is the event's lead, with the authority to pull rank when they need to. This lead, as well as needing the relevant contextual experience, must have the tenacity and charisma to garner support and inspire people to follow their lead.

The four core roles structure works for all events, from the smallest to the largest. Like a repeating fractal pattern, it can be scaled up or down as required. But why is this structure so important?

Having worked with almost every imaginable type of live event, regardless of its scale, type, sector or purpose, I have yet to find a structure that is so simple yet delivers so much.

Impact. A team with the relevant content and contextual experience, and the right support at the right time, will be focused on creating the most impact. They won't need to focus on the common yet completely unnecessary problems a team going through a learning curve or falling over its own structure would have to deal with.

Clarity. You, the team, and everyone else involved with the live event will know whom you need to turn to about any aspect of it.

Value. With this team structure in the right place at the right time, you will get the best advice and direction possible. With the right expertise comes the best value: value from producing an event that works as well as it can; value from a team able to coordinate a wider team efficiently; value from knowing how to extract the best from the supply chain, given the unique quirks of live events.

Low risk. It is rare for a live event to present a risk or problem that those with the relevant contextual experience can't foresee. The right team in the right place at the right time will mitigate most, if not all, likely financial, practical and operational risks as well as reputational risks.

You have probably noticed how often I talk about the core team being in the right place at the right time. When is the right time, though?

4

Decisions, qualified or otherwise, made at the genesis of a live event, tend to have a far greater impact on that live event than decisions made later.

Chapter 4

The Tipping Point

The Facts Of Live principles can and should be applied right from the start, when a live event is first conceived – which can be before you have any of the right people or experience available or on board.

We look at how the decisions made at the critical first stage of any live event's evolution are often the most important decisions you'll need to make, and typically have a far bigger effect on an event's impact, value and risk than those taken by anyone involved at a later stage.

What is the tipping point?

The tipping point, as I call it, is the point at which an idea for a live event tips from being unspoken or largely theoretical to something worth considering. It's the point in time when:

- A brand manager, marketing director or someone else within a brand decides they want to consider a live event to launch a new product or service
- An artist decides they want to go on tour or stage a concert
- A government decides it wants to bid for the rights to host a major sporting event
- Someone has an idea for a fundraising event and wants to make it happen
- A group decides that sitting around isn't achieving anything and wants to organise a (lawful) demonstration or rally
- Someone or a group decides they want to start a new event, be that a festival, sporting challenge, or conference series, for example

- A brand, government or organisation decides it wants to stage a summit or conference
- An organisation wants to look at the feasibility of a celebration, public event, publicity stunt or similar
- A brand or country wants to create a pavilion or exhibition stand at a major event, expo, exhibition or tradeshow

In other words, the tipping point is the point in time when a person, group of people, or organisation makes the jump from thinking about something live-event related to seriously considering it. By seriously considering it, I mean the person, group or organisation applies time, money, effort or resources to it. It is at an event's conception that *The Facts Of Live* becomes relevant.

Typically, the decisions people make in the minutes after the tipping point can have a far bigger effect on the impact, value and potential risks of a live event than almost any other decisions down the line. Small decisions that may seem innocuous at the time about whom to task with what, how to procure, how to start and what path to take rapidly expand into work streams, strategies, treatments and approaches. Like a plant, these work streams, strategies, treatments and approaches take their form from the seed that they grow from. Once they get to a certain size, it becomes difficult, if not impossible, in any practical sense to change their shape or form.

Typical approaches

I have mentioned other industries elsewhere in this book, using architecture and construction analogies as the terminology of the construction industry is familiar to most people. They have an accepted basic comprehension of how the construction industry works. Alternatively, if someone needs an operation, they know this starts with a visit to the doctor, and that there will be a surgeon and nurses involved. This never changes. If a country is going to war, most people understand the ranking system within the military. A film needs a producer and director, and many people have some concept of what's involved. If they need legal advice, they know they need a lawyer; if they need financial advice, they know they need an accountant or financial advisor.

If asked 100 people about these sectors or requirements, I'd get 100 similar answers as they are so widely understood. If, however, I asked 100 people how they would go about commissioning or producing a live event, what answers do you think I would get?

I would likely get a great variety of different answers. I might even get 100 different answers, and I know this to be the case because I have this conversation with people from all walks of life and in every imaginable type of organisation every day.

I get answers like:

- I'd ring an event management company
- I'd call you, Will
- We usually do everything ourselves, and given the event is so small, we will cope somehow
- We're creating a sporting event, so I'm going to call on the expertise of a world-famous athlete or Olympian
- I'm the artist, it's my work, so I'll produce the event my way
- I'd call my friend Sarah, I am sure she did something similar a while back

- We'd start an organising committee, it's what everyone does on major events
- Should we start a new company to offset the risk?
- We'll do some scoping work to figure out just what it's going to take
- We'll put out a Tender or Request For Proposal (RFP) to see what ideas and thoughts we get back from the market
- It's a pavilion, that's a construction project, we'll call some architects
- I'd call our advertising/sponsorship/communications/digital/branding/marketing/PR agency
- I'd get on to our HR team and they can hire the right people to do it in house

The list goes on.

All of the above would likely result in a live event of some sort. All would result in a different process, and some approaches would be better than others. With no common approach, though, how do you know what you're doing is the best approach? Are you relying on word of mouth? Are you relying on the experience of having done an event before? Are you relying on your experience within a specific sector? Are you assuming the approach you've always taken will yield the best results? Are you relying on hearsay?

Whether you're doing everything yourself on a small event, likely to need the support of others for a larger event, or needing the support of thousands for a huge event, you need clear direction if your live event is to be as successful as possible. If there are other people involved, which will be the case in all but the rarest of situations, they will need clear direction. If people are second guessing what's happening, reverse engineering over-complicated processes and going through unnecessary learning curves or trying to understand alien terminology, they will be spending more time sorting problems out than using their expertise where it's best placed.

Given the lack of any standard or common approach to or understanding of what's involved with the development and planning of live events, and the knock-on effect this can have, you need to make sure your actions at the tipping point have the right impact on your success. At the tipping point in most sectors or industries, people know exactly whom they need to turn to. There's a common comprehension. More importantly, perhaps, they also know that if they don't get the right expertise at the right time, delays or well-intentioned but ill-informed advice will be costly or painful.

The same is true when it comes to live events. If you need a live event produced, designed or created, it stands to reason that the people and services you need to get on board at the tipping point are those with the relevant content and contextual experience of having done something similar before. Their collective expertise must cover all of the four key roles we've outlined in the previous chapters.

While some people do manage to get the right people in the right place at the right time, what happens an awful lot of the time is that people start to work out what the best team, budget and plan of attack may be *before* seeking the relevant expertise. This is a little like trying to work out what concrete is best for your building's foundations before you've even appointed the architect. Get the relevant experts on board first, and they will be able to decide or advise on the best team, budget and plan of attack.

There are various reasons why many people don't have the relevant expertise available at the tipping point when they're looking to organise a live event.

Why relevant experience is so often missing

The first common obstacle to having the right people in the right place at the right time is knowing whom you need in the first place. To use a cliché, 'You don't know what you don't know'. *The Facts Of Live* aims to fill this knowledge gap.

The second common obstacle to getting the right people in the right place at the right time is that producing and developing events isn't generally seen as a recognisable skill or craft in its own right. Instead, it's something that many people attempt to do themselves, irrespective of their experience. Alternatively, they will call on people with relevant content experience and expect them to have an immediate grasp of the contextual issues necessary to produce a live event: a sportsperson producing a sporting event, a musician producing a concert, or a brand manager producing a product launch, for example. We discussed this point at length in the 'Anatomy Of Live Events' chapter.

For the purpose of *The Facts Of Live*, I am assuming you're not looking to do everything yourself, learn how to do everything yourself, or expect others with the wrong experience to do everything themselves. Instead, you are looking for live events to be produced and developed professionally, so I am detailing what you need, where you need it, when you need it, and how to get it.

If you are planning to use external expertise for your organisation's live event, another, and probably the most common, obstacle could be your organisation's procurement and governance guidelines or practices. It is extremely common, and almost seen as normal, for an organisation to want to know the cost of any live event before it engages anyone to start working on it. As a result, the entire live event, rather than just the necessary initial expertise, is procured by means of a turnkey competitive process, be that a tender, RFP or similar.

At one level, this logic is completely understandable: as a client, you want to buy something and want to know what it will cost so you can contract or order it. But if an event requires any degree of design and development, which is true of all but the most formulaic of events, this logic is flawed. This approach is effectively asking for an event to be developed so that a concept and cost can be presented before the event's been developed properly, in order to find people to develop it. Unless the event is formulaic, you're asking for a large swathe of the work to be done before anyone has been appointed to do it, and before anyone is in a position to know everything they need to know to undertake the work with proper due diligence.

It's like asking a selection of architects for their design for a building and the detailed costs before you've appointed them to design and cost it, so you can then appoint that architect to design a building and have it costed.

In order to find the people to design and plan the event, the organisation issues a tender or RFP asking the people who will develop and plan it what the live event will look like and cost before they've been appointed to develop and plan it. The procurement process then becomes an exercise in compliance with the tender or RFP rather than an exercise in developing an event that achieves the most impact and value, primarily because only the information in the tender or RFP is available, rather than the many and varied factors that will only arise once work starts in earnest, but will have a far bigger effect on the event's design and cost and the event's impact.

The end result of this process is that the people with relevant content and contextual expertise end up coming on board so long after the tipping point that, in most cases, the event's development already has a life of its own and is travelling along a certain path, irrespective of whether that path is going to result in an event that creates the most impact or returns the best value.

A final more subtle reason why many people or organisations don't call on relevant expertise at the tipping point is that it can sometimes be seen as a threat. If a team of people in an organisation is tasked to develop and produce an event, they may fear that asking for relevant expertise to help or guide them will put their own roles in jeopardy. After all, as they were tasked with putting the event together in the first place, they would presumably be considered competent and able. If people think the relevant experts may steal their limelight or pose a risk to potential bonuses or promotions, it is almost impossible to break through these subconscious obstacles.

In fact, it can be difficult even to be aware of these obstacles until it's too late, which is why it's so important that those at the top of the food chain, as it were, understand the skills and experience required to put together a live event that creates the most impact and returns the best value before they task anyone to do the job. At the very least, they need to ensure that there is the right balance between relevant contextual and content expertise and any other people who need to be involved but may not have the relevant experience.

Maximising impact

I was once asked to produce a high-profile product launch for a brand for what is now an extremely well-known product. I didn't feature in the development process until long after the product launch was conceived; long after the tipping point, in other words. The launch started life within the brand, perhaps in a boardroom, certainly during a high-level meeting somewhere. Those involved within the brand were keen to use a particular venue for the launch as it was a good fit for the brand.

The brand had initial conversations with the venue, and they reached an agreement. Meanwhile, the brand tasked its digital agency with creating various online strategies and content to support the launch. The brand's advertising agency started creating a graphic identity for the event and producing intriguing teasers, both online videos and press releases. Media partners looked at how the impact of the event could be amplified across TV and radio.

Inevitably, as work within the brand moved forward and the event began to take on a direction, everyone involved had more and more questions about the detail of the event – understandable questions. What would it look like? What form would it take? It was at this late point that the brand decided it had enough information to brief someone with event expertise to look at developing and producing the event in earnest.

A while later, via a process that took far longer than it needed to, I was in front of the brand as the person who would be producing the product launch event. To summarise what is a long and complicated, but surprisingly common, story, a number of issues came to light within the first hour of my involvement. The venue was completely inappropriate for the event's ambitions. It wasn't large enough to accommodate the number of people the brand needed to come close to justifying the cost of using it. But it was too late: the media already had the date and venue details, and the brand was adamant it didn't want to change the venue, which would have meant losing both face and the deposit it had paid.

The venue was set in stone, and so was the date, which was too tight to deliver the brand's ambition for its product launch. We've all had to work to tight deadlines, but the laws of time and physics do become an immovable reality at some point.

The online activity that the digital agency had designed was beautiful. I am hard to impress, yet even I was impressed with what they had achieved. The way in which the online activity was to link to the live activity at the event was impractical, though. Technically it was possible, which was probably the reason why no one had questioned it up until this point. But while it was technically possible, it was unrealistic due to the time we'd need to undertake the research and development, and then fabricate the new technology it would require.

The advertising agency had already released some of the product launch teasers to parts of the media, meaning that the design, format and style of event was also, to all intents and purposes, set in stone. The media partners (TV and radio) had started designing their coverage and engagement. This wasn't set in stone, but we would need to change plans completely, negating much of the work the media partners had done to date. What a lot of wasted time.

My task, among all of this, was to fashion an event late in the game that somehow answered the brief, helped everyone meet their conflicting agendas, did its best to work with the work that had been undertaken to date, and over and above everything else, actually launched the product to the media and public in a meaningful way. This being a common set of circumstances for us, I and the team I worked with came up with something that worked and that was, on the surface, impressive.

As is often the case with live events, the euphoria and excitement of the event itself and the relief of having delivered it masked the realities of its effectiveness: its impact. Had someone with relevant contextual experience been involved shortly after the tipping point, the impact of the event would have been very different.

Firstly, the venue. For maximum impact, the brand didn't really need the event to be at the location it had been so excited about. It simply needed its product to be seen there, which could have been achieved with a simple photoshoot, media moment or publicity stunt – an event in itself, yet exponentially smaller in scale, complexity and cost. This would have resulted in the same imagery the event created, yet for a fraction of the price. Imagine what the brand could have done with the money it saved. More marketing of that imagery, perhaps?

Secondly, we could have created an event for far less money that placed the product into the hands of a significantly larger number of people with no less impact and just as much drama and excitement. For maximum impact, we could have used a venue close to the venue for the photoshoot and media moment, yet not the inappropriate venue itself.

Another consideration is the fact that the time and money the brand spent with its advertising and digital agencies could have been dramatically reduced had those agencies had a clear brief, supportive direction and leadership from the outset. This is difficult to quantify in hard numbers, but the potential savings are obvious.

The final point, while less of a fundamental issue, is one of reputation. When engaging with media partners like TV and radio, a brand wants favourable exposure. To mess the media around, needing them to change their plans, isn't ideal. The media obliged on this occasion as the brand had a strong reputation, but it was a needless risk.

As a result, the event was a compromise, doing none of the things it had set out to do as well as it could have done them. It cost, I estimated, about 25% more than it needed to, with all things considered. Make no mistake, the brand was ecstatic with the result at the time – it was hard not be with the high drama, technological wonders and showmanship we delivered – yet closer analysis revealed that from a business and commercial perspective, it was a missed opportunity, and an expensive one. It had nowhere near the impact it might have had.

I have kept the brand and product details anonymous in this example, but scenarios like this are surprisingly common – often the norm. Many people in organisations and brands may not realise that the issues I've outlined above are even playing out, let alone that they are avoidable. If a brand is aware of these issues, it can make sure its people are focused on the bigger picture.

Understandably, a brand can feel exposed, both financially and reputationally, if it brings in live-event expertise at or just after the tipping point without a well-defined brief, but I can alleviate such concerns. The cost of this expertise can easily be capped or offset and straightforward legal agreements can be used to manage concerns about reputation and leaks that could theoretically occur through involving third parties. Then, just as an architect would work with a client to develop the needs and objectives of a building before designing it, or an advertising executive would work with a client to understand more about the product and the target audience before creating an ad campaign, qualified event experts can help a brand quickly cut through everything that doesn't matter and focus on what does to produce an event that meets whatever targets, ambitions or objectives the brand or organisation has.

The right expertise being in the right place at the tipping point is one of the biggest factors that will help produce an event with the most impact possible.

Maximising value

The value of a live event is perhaps the biggest variable that can be affected at the tipping point. The same type of event with completely different approaches at its tipping point can result in dramatically different results.

To illustrate this, I'm going to use the example of two major single sport events. The first was an event that I became involved with long after the tipping point, and the second was an event where I was involved from the tipping point onwards.

The first event had its origins deep inside a public sector organisation: a government body. At the tipping point, in this case when the sporting event got the green light, the organisation put a project board together: a group of people from the government, the sport and various consultants. The function of this project board was to provide governance and oversight to the sporting event.

One of the board's first tasks was, perhaps understandably, to undertake various pieces of consultative work and feasibility studies, in part to understand what was and wasn't possible. More subtly, this work also began to inform key stakeholders of the board's plans and mitigate any concerns.

As time progressed, the next step the board took was to form an organising committee that would report in to the board. The organising committee would be the group of people responsible for organising the event. 'Organising', I always find, is a strange word for such a committee, as there's a great deal more involved than just organising. Still, it's what these committees are named.

The organising committee was not headed up by someone who had produced or organised a similar event, or indeed any event, before. It was not headed by someone with relevant contextual or content experience, but by someone the board viewed as being a safe pair of hands. Someone who had successfully run a large department before was considered more than capable of running the organising committee.

The organising committee went on to hire or contract all the requisites of any solid organisation: lawyers, accountants, an HR manager, and plenty more besides. Then came the need to hire people who had been involved with similar events before.

This team, the organising committee, quickly swelled to dozens of people. While many of these people had been involved with live events before, none had the contextual experience of leading and running such an event. They'd always been part of a bigger team or had a consultative role previously.

While this team was more than capable of running an organisation, it didn't have the contextual experience to deliver the event. The committee therefore packaged up and outsourced these requirements to a variety of specialist companies and partners that had delivered similar or identical projects before. These organisations in turn used numerous subcontractors for the many and varied goods and services they needed for the event.

The end result was a board, an organising committee and its many advisors, specialist delivery partners, and subcontractors. With so many people involved, the event was an enormous success, applauded from all quarters, as it had become too big to fail. It was indeed a magnificent event, truly impressive. However, less publicly (at the time), there were two fundamental areas where this project didn't fulfil its potential. One was its efficiency and the other its value, which together dramatically reduced its potential impact.

I'll not focus too much here on the efficiency issue, save to say that with so many people involved, and both duplication of and gaps in roles and responsibilities, there were unnecessary complications and frustrations. While it's hard to quantify these complications scientifically, logically they can only lead to more wasted time and cost than is necessary.

The second issue, value, is easier to understand and quantify. The way this event was set up at the tipping point was typical of many such events the world over. It seems to be, after all, the most logical way of setting such an enterprise up – if you don't have the content and contextual experience of having done a variety of similar events before, or have only done so in a particular field or sector. Inevitably, though, this extremely common scenario involves a board on a learning curve, usually only used to doing things in one way. It involves an organising committee of extremely intelligent people who may have to learn contextual lessons as the project evolves. As the organising committee may well not have the relevant expertise on tap in house, this scenario

then involves a raft of specialist delivery partners who have produced or organised similar events before. These partners often have to spend their time advising and educating the organising committee and the board the committee reports to.

This is about as inefficient as an event structure can be, firstly because so many people are on a learning curve, and secondly because much of the work is duplicated between the organising committee and the specialist delivery partners before anything gets to the subcontractors who will undertake the work.

Precise numbers surrounding sporting events are always open to huge interpretation as it's so difficult to determine accurately what's included in or excluded from any budgets, people's time being the most open to interpretation. However, this event cost at least 50% more than it needed to by comparison to similar events that had gone before it. Some would argue it was well worth it because the event was such a huge success. Others would argue it could have offered far better value had it been run more efficiently, which would only have been possible with the right people in the right place at the tipping point. Without these experts in place at the outset, politics and processes can send events down an almost irreversible path extremely quickly.

Major sporting events specifically are often judged on, among other things, the economic impact they deliver to the city they are hosted in. Almost all sporting events have been demonstrated to return a hugely positive economic impact on cities, but I would argue that this economic impact could be far greater if the events were run as efficiently as possible, rather than in the way they are often run.

This is not a direct criticism. I have often been heavily involved at the heart of the process when governments and large organisations are trying to get major events in various sectors moving forward. It is not easy; in fact, it's a miracle many of them see the light of day at all with the amount of hoops we all have to jump through. What happens time and time again, though, is that insufficient relevant contextual expertise is either involved or even recognised as being necessary at the tipping point, or the most senior people involved adopt the approach that is most familiar to them, irrespective of its effectiveness or efficiency, relying on a model they have used countless times before and just assuming it's the most efficient and effective approach. And this is just as common for major events as it is for smaller events. People turn to whom they know, what they think is best, or what they've always done, irrespective of whether it's right or best practice.

There is an alternative, though. We'll use an example of another major sporting event here: one that I was involved with from the outset, not long after the tipping point.

I was invited to the first board meeting to discuss a major sporting event. It became clear during this meeting that every one of the fifteen or so people around the table had concerns they wanted addressing. Representatives were there from public sector bodies, the sport and other key stakeholders. Understandably, they all thought their concerns couldn't wait and needed addressing immediately. This is common.

What hadn't existed until this point was any contextually relevant structure or leadership – which was, in part, why I had been invited to the meeting: to look at what needed putting in place.

There were many teams and organisations that needed leading, each with a representative at the board meeting. Had they not been led with qualified direction, these representatives would have formed numerous committees to work out what to do and what may be best. Then, no doubt, they would have undertaken a raft of consultations and

feasibility work, which would likely have resulted in a great end result, but would have been an unnecessary use of time, money and resources.

Being involved at this early stage, soon after the tipping point, I was able to apply structure and direction to all activity. With the relevant contextual experience behind me, I already knew what would work, what wouldn't and had identified the few things that needed more consideration. I also knew how the concerns and requirements of those around the table would likely pan out as work progressed. All the representatives at that board meeting got what they needed: they had their concerns addressed, either immediately or with a clear plan to do so moving forward.

I then sorted out structuring and resourcing the organising committee (to use that popular term again). However, this organising committee consisted of just a handful of people, using the core team approach of four key roles. I was the lead, a representative from the sport took the content lead, and people with the relevant contextual experience led the physical delivery and the operations and logistics requirements. In turn, we then had commercial, sponsorship and marketing roles in place to work with this core team.

This handful of people had proven experience of having done similar or identical work before, negating the need for any learning curve in their respective areas. And they could see the job through. There would be no need for additional experts or specialist companies. The organising committee produced the event, and then contracted the goods and services it needed directly. The result was a streamlined, efficient and nimble machine that delivered a hugely successful event for a fraction of the cost, both in time and money, of the alternative.

The difference between these two events was not obvious at a surface level. Both events looked and were fantastic, yet value-wise, the difference was huge.

Figure 4.1 illustrates this more clearly.

The first example involved a board, an organising committee, specialist companies/delivery partners/ expertise, and subcontractors providing goods and services. This resulted in duplication of work, confusion over who was responsible for leading different activities, and the organising committee learning from the specialist companies they'd appointed.

The second example involved a board, an organising committee with the relevant expertise and experience within it, and subcontractors providing goods and services. There was no or much less duplication of work, everyone had clarity over who was responsible for leading different activities, and the organising committee had the right experience from the outset without the need to learn as they went along.

The first example is the approach adopted by a group of people finding their way as they go, while the second example is the approach adopted by a group of people with the necessary experience to guide and lead the way from the outset. Why form an organising committee that is then going to hire or outsource to companies to do the management and detailed planning (the organising) work? Why not form an organising committee with the relevant content and contextual experience from the outset? You will get similar results from either of these approaches, but the value each offers will be dramatically different, and with it the impact of the event. You can maximise the value of your live event simply by having the right expertise available at or soon after the tipping point.

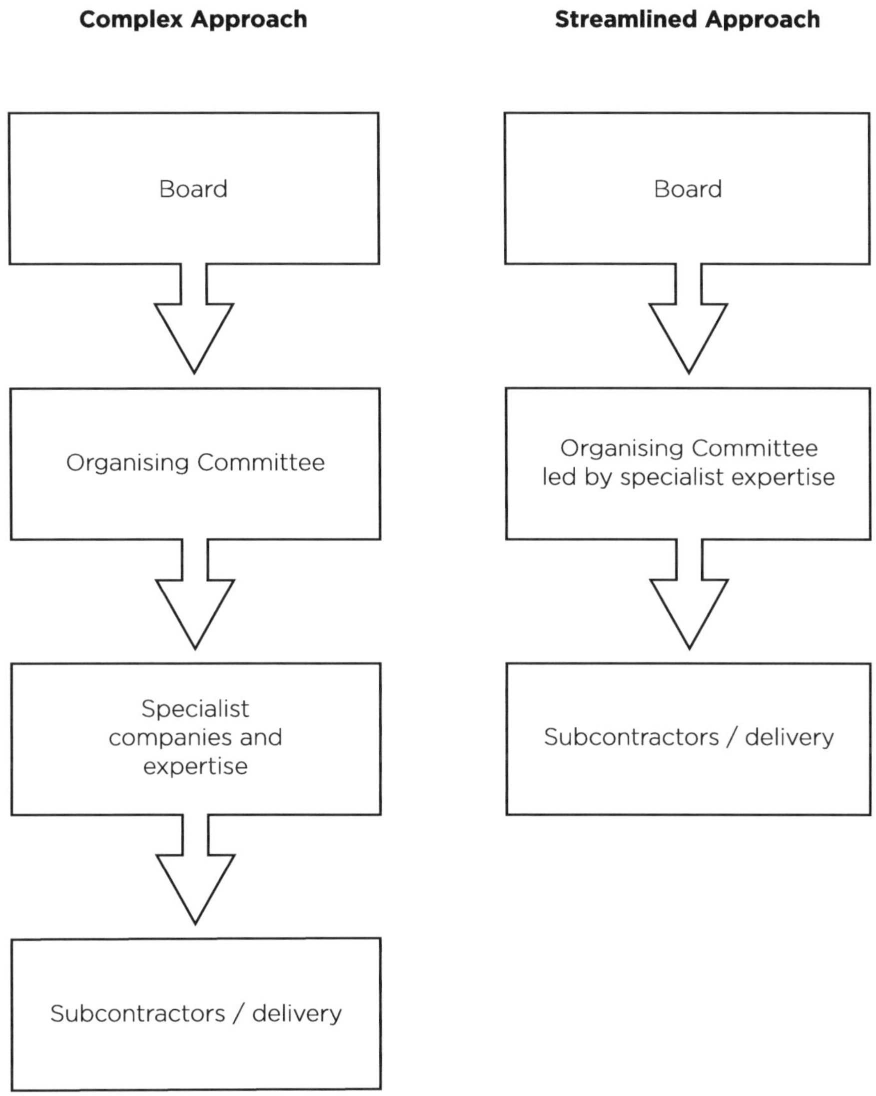

Complex Approach

Board

↓

Organising Committee

↓

Specialist companies and expertise

↓

Subcontractors / delivery

Streamlined Approach

Board

↓

Organising Committee led by specialist expertise

↓

Subcontractors / delivery

Figure 4.1: Major event organising committee approaches

Minimising risk

Another factor that can be addressed and mitigated at the tipping point is risk. Although risks come in many forms, they fit broadly into three categories:

- **Financial,** eg not having or raising enough money, and losing or running out of money
- **Physical,** eg injuries, physical damage, illness and 'acts of God'
- **Reputation,** eg bad news stories from perceived negligence, overspending, or concerns about the content or activity of an event

The examples I used in the previous section covered large-scale events, but the same principles apply regardless of the size of the event. In the interests of balance, I'll use a couple of examples of much smaller events to illustrate how risks can be mitigated effectively at the tipping point.

My first example is a live event for a relatively unknown brand. This brand wanted to exhibit its new product at a well-known exhibition (tradeshow) that was expensive to exhibit at.

A challenge with exhibitions is that a brand's aims can become muddled. Is the brand looking to sell more products, build brand awareness, broadcast certain messages into the public domain, meet its customers, or get its product into the hands of new consumers? Trying to do all of these can, and often does, lead to compromises, especially if a budget is tight.

This brand had a tiny amount of money, barely enough to pay the fees to exhibit, but it was adamant it wanted to exhibit at this event. Luckily, I ended up involved pretty much at the tipping point. Before the brand started trying to plan things or work out how to do the many and varied activities possible at an exhibition, I worked closely with the board members to understand what they were actually looking to achieve by being there, and challenged their objectives when I thought either they were unrealistic or they could perhaps achieve more.

It turned out that they were mainly looking for exposure and marketing opportunities. This new brand's directors didn't have any real expectations about selling their products or generating leads at the exhibition, especially as the product was still at the prototype stage. Knowing that, I advised them to focus on exposure and forget wasting what little money they had on trying to generate leads they didn't believe they were going to get, nor did they need at this point in time. We focused on creating an exhibition stand that did one thing and one thing well, its sole purpose being to get the brand noticed among the more established players around them who had millions to spend on their exhibition stands. We then programmed a series of activities and events to take place on that stand to get the brand further coverage over the course of the exhibition.

As a result, not only did the brand get noticed, it also gained numerous sales leads and partnership opportunities. All of this for a product that was only at a prototype stage.

As my team and I were involved right from the outset, we were able to help this brand avoid common risks.

Financial. With very little money to spend, had the brand adopted a traditional approach, which it would have done without guidance, it would almost certainly have overspent, posing significant financial risks to other aspects of its business. Alternatively, it would have tried to do everything on a budget rather than focusing on doing one thing well.

Had the brand put out a turnkey tender or RFP at the tipping point stage, it would have filled the tender with the many and varied requirements it wanted to achieve. The right experience on board at the tipping point could challenge and suggest alternatives to the board as part of an open, honest and detailed dialogue that wouldn't be possible, in any useful sense, as part of a competitive turnkey tender process. The tender or RFP approach would almost certainly have cost more money than was necessary, or even available in this instance.

Activities that would cost very little in the environment the team was used to working in would have cost considerably more to stage in a public space. My relevant contextual experience ensured their plans were amended to fit to a budget while maintaining the event's creative integrity and impact, rather than risking a huge overspend once the planning had reached the point of no return.

Physical. The original plans, while they looked innocuous enough on paper, would have resulted in serious overcrowding issues had the marketing plans not been adjusted. The original plans simply weren't suitable for the public space the event was intended to take place in. The unpredictability of the public coupled with the lack of space to warn or protect the public and those performing adequately presented a considerable risk of injury.

Reputation. Some of this new brand's investors and people in its industry were dubious about exhibiting at a prestigious event, fearing it would highlight the brand's inexperience rather than its selling points. The brand's reputation was, at this point in time, heavily reliant on good media coverage as it was new and still attracting investment.

Appropriate contextual advice at the right time, the tipping point, helped lead the brand in the right direction from the outset. It didn't make mistakes it could ill afford, ensuring its reputation was managed and remained intact throughout.

A second example of a small event where the risks were high was a piece of performance art in a public space to launch a new theatre production. The nature of the theatre production lent itself to an over-the-top and exuberant piece of performance art or a stunt.

The producers and management team of the theatre performance were well versed in staging theatrical productions within the confines of a stage in a theatre. This stunt, though, needed to be in a public space – a space the media would gravitate towards, recognisable in any television, print or online coverage, and inherently occupied by the public.

I wasn't involved with this publicity stunt right at the tipping point, but did get asked to help before plans had moved on too far, so was able to support the team and influence the best outcome. The team's plans and aspirations were considerable. And they had already asked various organisations to start looking at different activities and performances that could be included as part of the launch event.

Looking at it with the relevant contextual experience, I realised that the event would end up costing considerably more money than the team had to spend, it would pose enormous risks to the public in the area, and given the marketing campaign the team was proposing, more people would have wanted to come and watch than the public space could safely accommodate. The team's finances were at risk, but more importantly, perhaps, their reputation would have been at stake had anything gone wrong. Even a minor problem can be, and often is, amplified into a much bigger issue by the time the media have run and rerun the story.

Had overcrowding occurred, the media would have been reporting on the safety concerns rather than positive coverage of the launch of the theatre production. In fact, had there been too many people in this particular space, there would have been precious little space to accommodate the media, which would have resulted in no or less than favourable coverage.

I will freely admit that the team did not receive my advice well. 'What do you know?' and 'I'm sorry, we don't believe you, you are wrong' were remarks I heard a lot over the course of the initial meetings. This is common. Unfortunately, by the nature of what I do, I often have to explain delicately what isn't possible before getting to what is possible and best for the live event.

I worked through their concerns pragmatically, and I proposed various ideas and approaches that would deliver against their objectives while being affordable, generate the coverage they were looking for, and be both tangible and safe. I also knew what would and wouldn't get approved by the various authorities involved in an event held in a public space, how far we could push certain regulations and restrictions, and how to go about it sensibly.

The launch event went off exactly as we'd planned it. Having the right experience involved soon enough after the tipping point, the theatre production and management teams made sure numerous risks were mitigated.

Summary

In most walks of life, the actions and people required at the tipping point are clear. When you decide you want to build a house, that's the tipping point and you need an architect. But when it comes to live events, there are so many different views on who is needed when. As a result, people and organisations often don't call on the right expertise at or close to the tipping point.

The repercussions of the tiny decisions you make at the tipping point, be they good or bad, become amplified as time progresses. Therefore, having relevant contextual experience on board at the tipping point can drive an event forward to create the maximum impact possible. It can extract the maximum value from an event, saving huge amounts of money in some instances. It can also mitigate many risks, as almost all likely risks can be foreseen by those with relevant experience. Make sure you seek out the right expertise at an event's genesis.

Advising you to get the right experts on board at the right time is not enough, though. You also need to look at how to acquire this expertise in the most productive and powerful way possible.

The right expertise involves working with the right people. The success of a live event has a great deal more to do with people than processes or agreements. For that reason, you need empathy with what's involved in producing a live event to ensure you and your team are best prepared.

How does the unique combination of circumstances that live events exist in need managing and leading? What effect can producing live events have on the experts you need?

5

Live event leadership starts with empathy and ends with empathy.

Chapter 5

Leadership

Live events are all about people. It's people that make them happen. It's people that overcome the constant challenges and obstacles. It's people that will get your live event over the line.

No process, no software, no schedule and no contract will come anywhere close to the effectiveness that strong, authoritative and empathetic leadership will have on the success of your live event.

Leadership starts at the top. Even if it's not you actually leading the event, the people you bring on board to lead your event will, to a greater or lesser degree, be led by you in some way. And even if you're leading just a small element of a live event, you're still undertaking a leadership role.

We look at the key principles of live event leadership and the factors that underpin and empower successful leadership.

It's all about people

The information in this chapter is a little more subjective than that in the rest of *The Facts Of Live*. Distilled from two decades of work and research, it's just as relevant, though.

Live events are so reliant on how we humans work together. Without people working together well, the foundations, guidance and principles in this book will not be effective. Understanding, empathy and insight influence how you or those you bring on board set up any processes or formal arrangements and underpin how an entire team works together.

The right team is just the start, though. When approaching and working with live events it's tempting to adopt practices familiar from other disciplines and traditional project management techniques. Sometime this works, but quite often it doesn't. Remember that live events exist in a unique combination of circumstances.

For a start, we have a deadline that can't be moved. It's true that many traditional project management techniques have solutions to cover this, but the speed at which decisions need making regarding live events can scupper even the best-laid and most agile project management practices. Adding in further ingredients, like the fact that live events leave you completely exposed and the fact most people like to look good most of the time, means egos and self-preservation feature heavily though not always helpfully. Then creativity, passion, politics and a myriad of other factors can skew reality, making processes difficult to follow.

Finally, you or your team will likely be relying on things completely outside your control. You can manage these things or work around them, but it's impossible to control the weather, the public, transport, other organisations, acts of God, subcontractors failing, the media – there's an endless list of things that can and will affect you and everyone else involved in the production and delivery of the live event.

All of these factors when they're combined mean that as well as having the right people led by your core team, you need to be able to rely on certain philosophies, principles and behaviours – or as I call it, leadership – to deal with them effectively.

If you intend to outsource everything or hand everything over to others, you may be reading this and thinking that none of it is your concern. Nothing could be further from the truth. It's almost impossible to hand over a live event in its entirety. If it's your brand, product, message or art on show at a live event, you're going to be involved in some way, shape or form. Moreover, in order to make sure the teams of people you have working with or for you are making you or your content look as great as possible, you need to have empathy with what they may face.

This will mean two things. It will mean that you'll know what's going on, and some requests or information that may seem strange will have more context. It will also mean you are better placed to do whatever you can to make sure those around you have what they need in order to help you.

Even if you have all the money and resources in the world, they will not always get you the best results. Empathy can be worth its weight in gold. Your actions and how you deal with or support others can have an enormous impact. And empathy costs nothing, meaning that the topics we will discuss in this chapter are just as applicable to the smallest live event imaginable as they are to the largest.

Process and competency balance

People can have a tendency to 'process-ise' everything when it comes to live events. A fabricated word, I admit, but it works well to represent a common desire to schedule, analyse, track and audit everything and detail every decision, action and requirement. Fear of failure and a desire for certainty can often result in every element of a live event being engulfed by processes and paperwork, which potentially pose a bigger risk than the paperwork is trying to mitigate. It's just not possible. Where do you stop?

The difficulty with all this paperwork comes when reality hits. The speed at which live events evolve and the sheer number of moving parts mean that processes are at best continually changing, or at worst, and more commonly, post-rationalised later on and created simply to keep line managers, clients, stakeholders or other onlookers content – inherently pointless work, that someone (probably you) ends up paying for.

Some would argue that if you're not following due process, you won't have adequate resources for the live event. This is a valid argument, but if you were to document and monitor every single aspect and tiny detail of every live event, few events would ever see the light of day because of what this would cost and the timescales typically involved. Some activity does need a high level of supervision and process (or due diligence), particularly high-risk and safety-critical activity, but there needs to be a balance between process (or paperwork) and people with relevant competence. It's people who make live events happen, it's people who can make quick decisions, often with little more than gut instinct, and therefore it's people who will meet your live event's immovable deadline.

At the eleventh hour, when you are standing in a field, in a venue or on a stage, moments from going live in front of your audience, processes or contracts are not worth the paper they're written on. They are then useless in any practical sense. It is only people who are going to help you.

Let me share a quick example with you. I'd been leading an event that had a great many stakeholders involved. With money pooled from a number of parties, the organisers had a formidable and robust system in place to authorise and spend the money and assign resources to tasks as and when they materialised. This was a process that took at best a few hours, and more typically, a few days between a request being made and the cost for that request being authorised. Early on in the process, I pointed out that this was going to cause problems down the line. Despite fighting my corner, I was disappointed to see my argument fall on deaf ears. After all, what did I know?

The afternoon before the event, some key participants suddenly realised, or decided, that they would need a change to the venue if they were going to participate. This change was relatively simple to put in place, but the people involved in making the change would need a firm instruction and order (commitment to pay) pretty much immediately. This was impossible though, because of the processes that the organisers had insisted upon. By the time the payment was authorised, it would have been far too late to change the venue, and that would have jeopardised the entire event.

What followed was panic and chaos within certain quarters. We wasted a good few hours trying to get the relevant authorisations in place so the work could move forward. The reality was that we had to circumnavigate systems and governance as soon as the requirement was identified, which was long before approval was granted, then we took care of the paperwork after the event. There was so much time and money wasted in doing so, though.

Tales like this are common, almost normal. Many traditional approaches and systems simply don't work in a live event environment.

It will, with some live events, be necessary to have considerable governance. This can range from simple self-imposed checks right the way up to entire committees, boards or even governments overseeing all activity. And there will, of course, need to be some processes set up to administer this oversight, but it's important not to get carried away. Typically, people, not pieces of paper, have the most up-to-date information in a fast-moving and evolving environment.

The balance between process (paperwork) and competency (people with proven and relevant experience) is easy to skew too far in either direction. People used to detailed project management, financial or legal due diligence can slow a project down with too much focus on process. People averse to any oversight or processes at all can miss things or, worse, put money, the live event, or even lives at risk. What's important is to put qualified or experienced overseers (the core team I've outlined) in place rather than micro-management. Are the key issues and requirements covered? What really matters? What are the key risks? It is around these questions that processes need to exist. For everything else, you rely on competency.

I will freely admit this is sometimes a contentious viewpoint. But having worked on some of the highest profile and most complex live events in history, along with some of the smallest, I know the things that put the most pressure on people and cause some of the most severe problems are ill-conceived processes, traditional project management approaches, and paperwork that serves no practical purpose. These are also the issues that end up costing brands, clients and organisations considerably more money than they need to, given they do little to serve the end result. Understanding of and empathy with the experiences and reality people face when they're involved in producing live events need to be the focus of how systems and processes are set up and run.

The process and competency balance is not always easy to achieve, but it is made a great deal easier with the right people in place.

This is another reason why the key roles we've identified, assumed by people with the relevant content or contextual experience, will lead everything else. Rather than have processes and governance set up by people without live-event-related contextual experience, make sure you have the core roles in place right from the outset. They can then establish or guide the governance and processes required.

Dictatorial leadership and democratic management

Here, I use the term 'dictatorial' affectionately. I've never found a more appropriate word in this context, though.

When you're creating and planning your live event, you're likely to have a team of people who need to work together, just as you would in any other walk of life. To perform well, these people need to work in a fair, open, encouraging and motivated environment. They need to feel comfortable airing their ideas and issues, knowing their opinions will be considered. This is how people in positive, modern environments are happy working. It's a democracy. As it should be.

Democracy is all well and good. It does, however, have one huge drawback. This drawback is hitting your fixed deadline, which live events typically have. If good, proper and democratic working practices mean you're missing key milestones, or worse, your final deadline is at risk, a democracy is the opposite of what

you need. Perhaps you're finding your teams aren't making decisions and taking action fast enough, possibly because all the information they need doesn't exist yet, or people want more time to make the 'right' decision or aren't empowered to make decisions. As a result, your live event is at risk of either failure or not living up to its potential. You don't have time to mess around. While the best decision may not always be possible, you do need a decision of some sort, and you need it immediately. Delaying everything until later puts more and more pressure on people, which does neither you nor your team any favours as you try to meet your final immovable deadline. It is at these moments that democratic management needs replacing with dictatorial leadership – strong, decisive, qualified and authoritative leadership.

Many people will argue that they are not authorised to make a decision without consulting everyone, or getting approval from everyone, or getting every version of reality from everyone. These may be valid claims. But dictatorial leadership decisions are judgment calls, and they need to be made by people both empowered and responsible to do so, typically with imperfect and incomplete information.

Dictatorial decisions can be made by anyone leading a particular part of a live event. The overall event lead may make a decision that affects the entire project. A department or area lead may make a decision that affects their area of responsibility. The people in these positions should have enough content or contextual experience to assess the information they do have (if any) and make a judgment call. There may be people around them who don't like the decision, there may be people above them who don't like the decision, but as long as they have the best intentions and focus on the live event's objectives, they must be empowered to make the decision.

I was once producing a large brand and marketing event, or publicity stunt as some called it, to take place live simultaneously in many countries on different continents. The event had many moving parts and an extremely nervous client. There were key elements to this multimillion-dollar venture that needed manufacturing, without which the event would have failed.

Given how important these particular elements were, the client was extremely anxious to get them right. Perfect, even. The design needed to be right, the price needed to be right, and the finish needed to be right. As a result, many people involved in the event were reluctant to sign off the price, design and finish until every single detail had been analysed, considered and debated, and then they wanted each detail signed off by a great many people.

As time marched on, the manufacturing and shipping deadlines were becoming more constrained, but getting the various clients to approve what we had proposed was proving difficult. They just wouldn't commit as there were so many levels of governance and everyone was afraid of making wrong decisions. But the event definitely had to go ahead. The publicity was out in the public domain, and the event not going ahead would have been an international PR disaster.

In the end, because I couldn't get approval in time on these particular items, I decided to authorise their manufacture regardless, without the budget or client approval. This was clearly high risk. On one hand, I was leading a multinational event for a global brand, and I would have been amazed if I'd got paid if it hadn't gone ahead, despite contracts being place. On the other hand, a key element of the event simply had to go to manufacture, but I couldn't get approval for it.

People who have not been in this position may simply look at this situation and say that with the right paper trail, my team and I could have effectively downed tools until we got the approval we needed. This, on paper,

would make perfect sense. However, we knew the event had to go ahead. Cancelling it wasn't an option and would have caused bigger reputational and commercial repercussions for me, my team and the brand. Between a rock and a hard place, I needed to make a decision. No meeting or committee was going to solve this. I decided to get the items manufactured.

In time, the client did approve the requirement, and was surprised and irritated to find out that I had already moved forward without their approval. Had the client decided not to approve the items, I would of course have had to own up and deal with the consequences.

I made a judgment call. I had to make a decision without enough information. It was a difficult call to make, but had I not made it, others on the team would have had to come up with another solution that would have likely cost a great deal more time and money, and put the entire team under a great deal of additional pressure.

The event would have been worse off and everyone involved would have had far bigger problems to solve.

This situation flies in the face of many project management traditions and may seem ridiculous. But when you're faced with real-time pressures, egos and the realities of dealing with complex organisations, scenarios like this – and ones where the risks aren't just commercial but safety or security related too – are common.

It's important that people leading an event or part of an event have the experience to make difficult decisions, and that they are supported when they do so. If you're working on a small event and there's just you involved, then the dictatorial leadership approach is far simpler. It's no less relevant, though. You'll need to make sure you make timely decisions, even if you don't have all the information you require.

At the end of the day, you have to deliver something, usually to a fixed deadline. The balance between dictatorial leadership and democratic management needs to be made with respect, of course. Being dictatorial doesn't mean you have to be cruel, insensitive or loud. It merely means you are authoritative and decisive. Empathy with the people who'll be carrying out the actions your decisions force is as important as making the decisions, if you want the decisions to be actioned.

Some people argue that fast-moving live events need a complete dictatorship: a leader who administers instructions to those beneath them. But this requirement is rare and best avoided. If your timescales are extremely tight and your challenges are formidable, it may be the best option, but make sure you or those you bring on board lead sensitively and respectfully. Understand what everyone involved in bringing the event to fruition may be going through as timescales and pressures can sometimes warp even the simplest of tasks out of all proportion.

Pressure

There's a common phenomenon that occurs during the development of live events. It's the compression effect, where time can warp many people's realities. In broad terms, as an event date nears, the amount of tasks that need doing increases, yet the time anyone has to complete those tasks diminishes rapidly.

Take a look at the graph in Figure 5.1.

At the tipping point, you will only know a few of the tasks that are necessary or that you will consider to be necessary to produce and deliver your live event. This is fine as there is still plenty of time to complete them. As time progresses, though, the number of tasks that you and your teams need to deal with will increase, escalating rapidly, exponentially in some cases. It is extremely unlikely that the number of people involved in producing the event will increase at the same rate as the number of tasks. This means that the time people have to complete the tasks diminishes, slowly at first, then severely as the event deadline approaches.

Those who are experienced with live events understand this well. Intellectually, those who haven't been involved with live events understand it, too. It's easy to comprehend: as time passes and workloads increase, it becomes harder for people to find the time to complete the work either to the level they would like, or at all.

As an event nears, everything, in the eyes of someone, becomes urgent. But rarely are many things truly urgent. As the deadline approaches, perceived uncertainty, worry about everything being ready on time, people's egos, politics, changes and a myriad of other issues produce a perfect storm. Panic, fear and excitement in this environment have different effects on different people. What almost always happens, though, is that suddenly everyone needs something, and they need it now.

It can become difficult to register or acknowledge all the issues that need dealing with, let alone action all of them, or even any of them. This is not

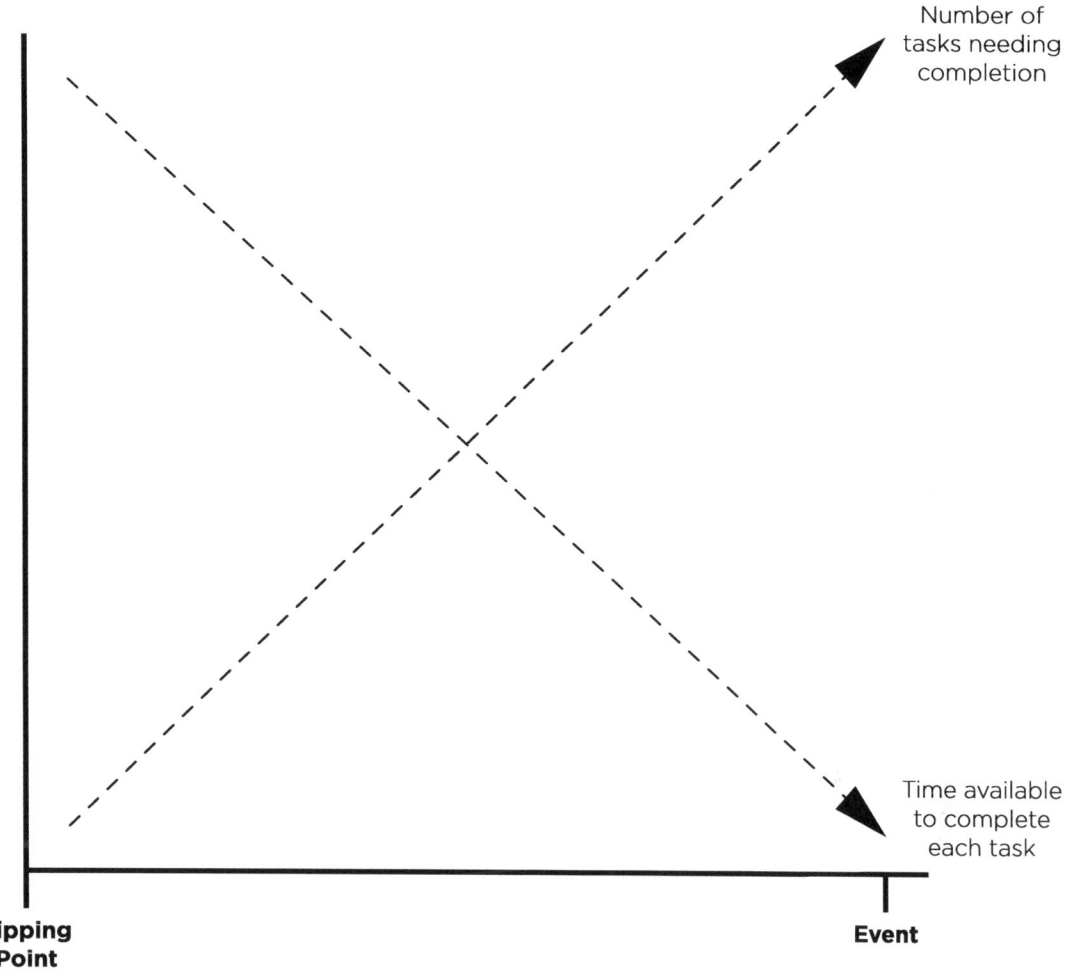

The number of tasks requiring completion escalates rapidly as an event approaches.
The time available to complete those tasks diminishes just as rapidly.

an exaggeration written for dramatic effect. On some events as the event date nears, I actually request that if anyone has an urgent need, they phone me. If they send me an email, they cannot assume I've received, read or actioned their request. Those who matter know this, and I have a structure in place to deal with anything else.

I am not suggesting this is always the best approach, but if your inbox receives hundreds of emails or requests an hour, no human alive can read them all, let alone action them. If the issue is real, it needs addressing sensibly. The art as the event date approaches is recognising what is important and what isn't, and having a structure in place to deal with it. This is an art that those who are used to producing live events become adept at. That's not to say they are immune to pressure, which is why it's always useful for everyone involved, even if indirectly, to have awareness of and empathy with the pressures people are under, and the effects these pressures can have.

In the period of time leading up to a live event, contracts, lists of roles and responsibilities, and similar formal paperwork are of little practical use. At this stage, you are almost entirely reliant on the people involved already being able to deliver. You can put safeguards in place along with backup personnel if yours is an extremely high-profile event, but fundamentally, your team will need to deliver.

Empathy becomes critical at this point. You need self-awareness of how you are talking to people and how, in turn, those people are reacting and going about their work. No matter how professional or experienced someone is, anyone can have a bad day. If, in addition to that bad day, they are under extreme pressure caused by the event requirements, it won't take much for them to snap. You don't want anyone snapping.

People don't always believe me when I say this: if I am leading an event, most of my time is spent not on sorting out event details, but on checking everyone is OK. I'm doing this pretty much constantly. From clients (when I'm in an agency environment) to members of an organisation (when I'm client-side) or to stakeholders, through to my own team, the supply chain and everyone working on the event – no matter how menial a person's task may appear, I care. I care because I care, but I also realise that it's people who will get the event over the line. Even if I don't necessarily like someone or believe they are doing their job as well as they could, it doesn't matter. They are involved in the event and therefore need treating with care and support.

If I ask someone to do something, I will be checking if they are able to complete the task and asking if they need support or have enough time and resources. If I see or suspect anyone is suffering or struggling, I offer them help. If someone refuses help yet clearly needs it, I will almost always develop a contingency plan in the background, just in case.

If you have a team of people working on an event, an awareness of the pressures they may be under as time compresses will serve you well.

Most live events inevitably involve both experienced professionals and those who may not have been directly involved with producing and delivering live events before. It is, in my view, absolutely impossible to tell what effect the pressures unique to live events will have on people until they are in it and it is happening. In my experience, I would say it's about a 50/50 split between those who cope and those who don't.

Ironically, perhaps, people who are typically super-organised and conscientious can find it hard to cope with live-event pressure as they tend to have perfectionist traits, and there comes a point in time with a live event where it's just not possible to execute everything perfectly. This can play havoc with their minds as they feel they are not doing their job properly and/or become fearful of reprisals. Those who are not that detail orientated can sometimes fare better under pressure as, typically, they neither see nor want to focus on details, so the pressure has less of an effect. In truth, though, it's impossible to gauge until an event nears. This makes it even more important to have empathy with what people may be going through and have the support in place to help should issues arise.

The effects of the time compression of a live event and the pressure that comes with it manifest in five different ways. You need to be aware of them all.

1. No effect at all. Those used to producing live events, typically those who are experienced event professionals, will likely feel no effect from the pressure at all. They expect the pressure and know how to deal with it, though that can change in an instant given the wrong set of circumstances.

2. Mistakes. The compression of time and the increasing number of tasks that need addressing can lead to people making mistakes. If this happens, the circumstances around the mistakes and the support, or support structures for larger events, around the person or people making them need to be looked at first. Immediately blaming or reprimanding the individual, most likely someone you are going to need to carry on working on the event, will cause more issues than it solves. They need to be approached sensitively and supportively.

Negligence is a different issue entirely. If someone is negligent, that needs dealing with accordingly. I am merely talking at this point about people making honest mistakes.

3. Lack of awareness. Some people – and yes, it happens – can drift through the production and delivery of an event completely unaware that there are any issues at all. Whether you would want such individuals working on an event again is something you would need to assess at a later date. As an event nears, whatever these people are not doing or dealing with needs a new owner or solution. Training someone or developing someone's self-awareness close to an event deadline may, conceivably, be possible, but you don't have time to find out and there are usually quicker ways to solve the problem. Time is your most precious commodity at this stage.

4. Denial. Denial is interesting to watch. It usually only manifests in people who have never worked on an event before or who lack relevant contextual experience, but are thrust or volunteered into a senior role to support a project and/or have been given a role considerably higher than their pay grade. Complete denial is rare, I admit, and only tends to happen on complex events.

Denial occurs when those responsible for areas of activity that are clearly about to go wrong to a trained eye deny that anything is wrong and insist everything is in hand. People in denial will typically say, 'It will be fine', 'There's no need to worry', 'I've worked in this sector for years' and similar without any information to back up their convictions. Unless they can provide or articulate concrete evidence that the tasks really are in hand, they are in denial.

Denial, in my view, is rarely due to anything underhand. It is more commonly due to the individual being petrified about the enormity of their task and considering their job or position – that they likely performed excellently prior to the event, and no doubt will continue to perform excellently after the event – will be at risk if they fail. Or they see asking for help or advice as a sign of weakness that will threaten their reputation or position.

Denial is the hardest of the five issues to deal with. You can rectify the others without necessarily involving or removing the individual involved, but someone in denial usually has quite a senior role, so removing them or suggesting there are problems can have repercussions. However, denial needs addressing head on. Short of removing the individual who is in denial, which may or may not be possible, depending on how senior they are, I have only ever found one solution for dealing with someone in denial close to an event date.

The solution involves having someone who is perceived to be as senior as the individual in question and who has proven, demonstrable content or contextual experience supporting them. This is a doubling up of resources and can have numerous repercussions. It's therefore best, in my view, to try to avoid this happening at all by making sure from the outset that any senior roles are filled with people who have performed the role before under similar pressures, or at least have similar experience: relevant content or contextual experience in line with their roles on the event.

5. Collapse. Someone collapsing completely, be it physically or just wanting to give up, is rare, but it does happen. I have seen both seasoned professionals and novices crack under the pressure they perceive themselves as being under. It happens, in my view, when the structure around them isn't set up correctly.

These collapses may be due to non-work-related issues that get exacerbated by the pressures of an event: pressures that the person in question may otherwise be used to. Collapse may also be due to a complete novice being unsupported or left unchecked.

If you are close to your team, you can sometimes spot and address collapse before it happens. If you're not close to your team, an empathy with the pressures people may be under as they work to produce and deliver your event will go a long way to helping you to prevent any issues that may be bubbling away just beneath the surface. If your team know you care, they will also highlight people they think are at risk, whereas if you're perceived as someone who doesn't care, news of these problems may reach you far later than it would otherwise. Such issues are extremely hard to quantify, but as you or your team are so reliant on people, and given you only have one chance to get a live event right, the wellbeing of your team as tasks mount up and time evaporates is paramount.

A little empathy can go a long way.

Quarantine chaos

I say it often: when you're dealing with a live event, you are rarely in control of everything that contributes towards its success. Curveballs are inevitable. Things will change. Change is the only certainty. In twenty years, I have never been involved with an event that has not continually evolved and changed. Trying to stop or prevent this change is a pointless task. You cannot control everything. It's just not possible.

Dealing with this change and the curveballs caused by anything from the public and weather through to egos and politics is where the art rather than science comes in. Against a continually changing backdrop, you have a live event that needs to happen on a certain date. Your most efficient path from the tipping point to the event is in a straight line, unencumbered by change and curveballs, as in Figure 5.2 (a). This straight line is your easiest, most enjoyable and likely most cost-effective, highest-value route to glory and making the biggest impact.

However, a live event is never going to evolve along a straight line. Change will happen; the live event will evolve. And as if that's not complicated enough, the distractions and issues caused by the event's evolution will be amplified by the fact changes are often thoughts, ie, potential changes, before they become definite changes. Unmanaged, the ifs, buts and maybes can rapidly transform change into chaos. This chaos can only result in one thing: curveballs that delay your progress, as in Figure 5.2 (b).

Delaying your progress is clearly not an option, as most live events have immovable deadlines. While these curveballs will happen, they needn't knock you off course. You may not be able to control everything or prevent chaos, but you can certainly manage it.

The deadline is fixed, so you or your team need to focus on what is set in stone until such time as any new or different requirements become both definite and feasible.

When you have the right team in place with the relevant content and contextual experience, they will be able to separate fact from fiction, and potential or possible from what's definite or confirmed right now. By quarantining any chaos, shielding it from those who are focused on what is definite, you can ensure your straight line remains intact, as illustrated in Figure 5.2 (c).

It is better to have a focused team doing the best they can than have them distracted by chaos and potential change, risking failure or poor quality. It's a great theory, but how does this work in reality? I'll answer that with a real-life example.

Planning had been underway for months for a major live event I was leading. Close to the event date, someone came up with the idea of adding about eighteen live sites all over the city the event was being hosted in: areas where people could gather and watch the event on large outdoor screens. This would have many benefits and on paper seemed like a good idea, but in effect, it meant another eighteen events needed producing and delivering.

This was no mean feat to pull off in the timescale we had available to us. Was it actually possible? Could we get permission to use the land we'd need? What would it cost? Was the money even available to do it? Where would the equipment come from, bearing in mind that equipment was already in short supply? How would these additional events be produced and delivered? Who would do this?

At the time, a team was already working towards a fixed deadline, focusing on what was confirmed and had to happen, without fail. I could have asked this team to jump on to producing the live sites: an unconfirmed and as yet non-thought-through requirement which would have added considerably to their workload, jeopardising the work they needed to focus on. Given the number of people we would need to involve to make the additional eighteen sites a reality, the team would soon have become unclear on what was confirmed and what wasn't. People from many quarters would have had questions that although simple to answer, would still have taken time, immediately tying up my team. In no time at all, chaos, of a sort, would have ensued.

Instead, I quarantined the potential chaos. There was no way on earth I was going to have my team distracted, likely wasting time and money. I wanted them focused on what they were already doing. Even though many on my team wanted to help and some had even started working on the feasibility, I put a stop to this. There was too much at risk.

Given I had the relevant contextual experience, I made some initial enquiries. I looked at why and whether these live sites were necessary and whether they were the right solution and set about getting agreements in principle from the landowners. I made some decisions about the design and the equipment we would require and enquired about where it may come from, identified the resources to produce and manage these new requirements, and created some ballpark budgets. I considered the knock-on effects and how they would impact the other activity. Making sure the money was available to deliver these live sites, I created an outline plan to move forward.

In brief, I worked out why, what and how, so it was clear to everyone. I then secured commercial approval. All of this happened quickly. Importantly, I could hand a considered instruction to the team to move forward. No fuss, no drama, and the straight line between the tipping point and the deadline stayed straight. Nothing was put at risk. A large curveball that could have caused chaos was quarantined.

To give you an example of a much smaller event, consider a community festival I was once involved with. With plans well advanced, the

Figure 5.2 (a): Your easiest path is a straight line without curveballs or interruption.

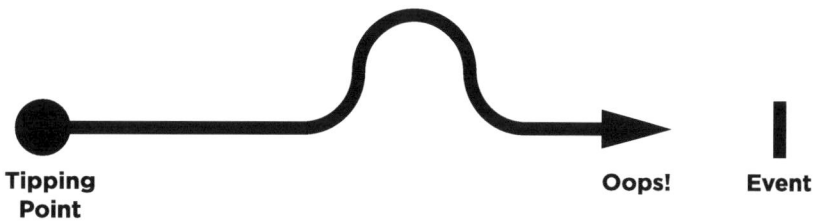

Figure 5.2 (b): Curveballs and change are unavoidable. Left unchecked, you risk all or part of your live event missing the deadline or being compromised to meet the deadline.

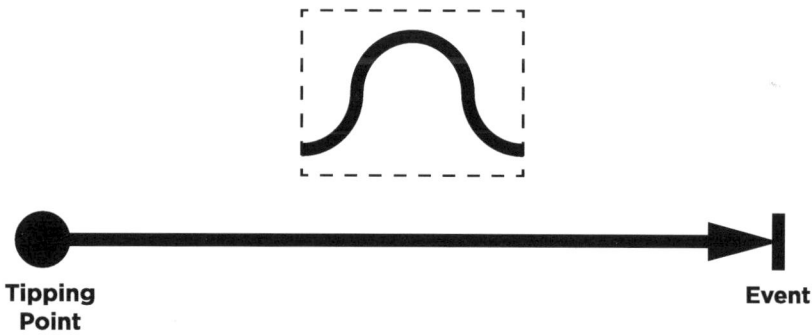

Figure 5.2 (c): Quarrantining the chaos - separating it and shielding it from those responsible for the core work - means it can be managed without affecting or risking the deadline: your live event.

Figure 5.2: Quarrantining chaos

event was due to be hosted in a particular location. The stakeholders and clients involved were keen to attract more people to the festival, though, and wondered whether it would be possible. I concluded quite quickly that this would be almost impossible in the proposed location, but recognised there was the potential to attract more people if we held the festival in a different location.

Moving the festival of course came with challenges. It would throw most of the planning to date up in the air. This was merely an idea, though, so before the team involved ran around trying to work out how to start again, complaining, wasting time and generally panicking, I quarantined the potential chaos. We had a deadline to hit, and if the new venue didn't become a reality, the festival still needed to happen on the given date in the original location, so I didn't want the team distracted.

Again, I was the person leading the project and I had the correct contextual experience, which is of vital importance. I was able to look at the proposed new site to check it was a feasible location and that we would be welcome. It was, and we were. I then looked at how the existing plans could be transferred, with only slight modifications, on to the new site. I looked at how the budget would be affected and created a clear plan to move forward.

Discussing this with the stakeholders and clients involved, I came to an agreement with them to proceed with the new plan. I then, and only then, instructed the team working on the project to change the plans. There was no drama as I handed over a clear plan of attack, and little of the work they'd done to date was wasted. Clear leadership.

It is not just major issues that can be quarantined like this; any number of issues that may cause chaos need to be quarantined. If you or your team are dealing with artists or personalities who are exceptional at their craft or talent, their inherent passion can overspill and affect an entire team if it's not managed, or quarantined, appropriately. Security risks, weather incidents, public transport issues, key talent or personnel not turning up on time, safety issues...all are examples of things that do happen and can cause chaos, yet needn't.

It's not just the person leading a live event who can quarantine things. Anyone involved needs to minimise the impact of curveballs that come along on those working for them. It is a key part of managing any live event or part of a live event.

Chaos is unavoidable, but it needn't affect people or your live event.

One plan, one schedule

There was a time when some colleagues of mine threatened to have T-shirts made with a phrase I kept repeating, which had almost become a catchphrase: 'One plan, one schedule'.

There are various schools of thought on how different people think and learn. Some learn through being taught, some learn by seeing things visually, and some learn through experience. I am no education expert, yet I always maintain that if people can see something, they will comprehend it far more quickly.

When it comes to live events, five questions are about as fundamental as they come:

- What is the event?
- Where is it to take place?
- When is it to take place?
- What's the schedule?
- What is it or what does it look like?

For any event, from the smallest to the largest, some version of a plan, be that a diagram showing where the live event is to take place within a venue or location, or a rough drawing of what it will be, can exist right from the tipping point. It may be vague or incorrect, but a visual plan, however uncertain, for people to look at gives them something tangible to agree or disagree with. I have produced a plan using a Sharpie and a cardboard box before. Not the most elegant solution, but when I'm faced with a roomful of blank faces and the only surface to draw on is a box, the scribbles I produce with a Sharpie save a considerable amount of time.

In all but the rarest of cases, there will be more than one person involved in producing a live event. Within an event's fluid and evolving environment, everyone involved can find not knowing what's going on to be a key frustration. However, it's extremely common for multiple versions of plans, documents and schedules to exist. This is no great surprise: different people and organisations need to know what they are doing and organise themselves in their own way. This is normal. However, all these people are producing one live event. Therefore, there can only be one version of reality, one plan (or set of plans), and one schedule (or set of schedules) for everyone involved in the event to use as a reference point. People can then create their own schedules for their own work and activity, but there must be one central reference point against which any other documentation is based. One plan, one schedule.

This may sound obvious, but in my experience, it's rare that it happens. Even if there are only two organisations involved, a client and an agency, for example, it's extremely common for the client to have their own version of things and the agency to have another, at least in the early days of any development. Then different parties come on board at different times, creating their own version of reality as they become involved. Increase the complexity of

an event from two parties to dozens, or hundreds, or thousands even, and the issues expand. Each party will have their own way of doing things, but all need to be referencing the same source information.

On nearly every project I am involved with, I sound like a scratched record. If I find anyone creating a new reference plan or schedule, they'll hear me saying, 'One plan, one schedule.'

I was brought in to lead a product launch once: a live event dressed up as a concert. There were to be a few component parts: a concert with A-list acts; an exhibition showing off the product being launched; a party for some VIPs. There would also be a radio station broadcasting live with its own elaborate set-up, and a small TV station would be broadcasting live, too. All straightforward enough – or, it should have been.

Before I got involved, the project had been drifting forward for a few months, gradually building momentum. The brand involved had appointed individual organisations to look after each element pretty much in isolation from each other. However, all of the elements had to come together as one integrated event. The people attending – the brand's audience – would only see one event, so it needed to be seamless for them.

Having been called in to sort out the concert element, I started asking a few questions. Simple questions like when things would be happening, the timings of the event, and where everything would be happening. Unsurprisingly, each organisation involved gave me a slightly different version of reality. I was given, either verbally or in writing, the schedule for the exhibition, the party, and the radio and TV broadcasts. All seemed to conflict with each other. When I asked for a plan – anything to show where various things were going – I received nothing. Everyone told me that no plans existed as the planning was still at an early stage.

When I hear this, it rings alarm bells. Even though the event was in its early stages, the individual teams had been working on whatever they were doing without direction for months. Whether the organisers realised it or not, this was going to cost the brand considerably more than was necessary as much of the work would need to be redone. With everyone working in silos without clear direction, they were inevitably going to be wasting time and effort, causing frustration.

Before starting on the concert side of things, which was what I had been brought in to produce, I created a plan and a schedule for the entire event: every element. This was quite literally a sketch on a piece of paper and a crudely thrown together schedule based on my interpretation of the four conflicting versions of reality I'd been given. I then sent this to everyone involved, including the brand, spouting my 'one plan, one schedule' mantra – in a polite way, clearly! I pointed out that if we were going to create a live event that would actually deliver what the brand wanted and that we could all be proud of, it needed a clear direction.

I explained to everyone that the plan and schedule I'd sent round would be the foundation on which all activity would be developed: the reference point for everyone. No matter how many people were involved or how many more would become involved, they would all refer to the one plan and one schedule. They were free to create their own plans and schedules for their own use, but the one plan and one schedule would be the reference point.

Everyone fed in their thoughts and opinions on the plan and schedule I had created. I reconciled these opinions and sense checked everything, and within a matter of days, we had a plan and schedule that, by and large, remained unchanged throughout the process of producing and delivering the event, and gave everyone the momentum they needed to move forward efficiently and far

more happily. The clarity these two simple documents offered meant everyone suddenly had direction. Moreover, the brand knew what it was getting, too. The plans became tangible rather than just talk and ideas.

I clearly have plenty of experience necessary to produce live events, but this doesn't mean a version of the plan and schedule couldn't have been created by someone without experience at the outset of the project. It would have given everyone far more focus and would have avoided three months of aimless activity and the waste it caused. This illustrates the importance of having these two key documents.

Of course, large events, where the activity is complex or running for a long time, may need a whole plethora of plans and schedules. Even then, though, you need one set of reference plans and one reference version of a schedule. A live event often means informing more and more people about the plans and schedules as each new party becomes involved. When you're talking to someone for the first time, you need to realise that after your explanation, they may still not comprehend what is happening, even if they say they are sure. You need to be sure they are sure, so you need

something you can show everyone at every stage of an event's lifecycle, right from the tipping point.

One plan, one schedule. This one leadership initiative will cure all manner of evils, and prevent many others from ever appearing.

Summary

Live events are above all a people and emotion-led business. Understanding what those you bring on board need and may go through will inherently lead to better results.

A team needs strong leadership: leadership that knows when to step in and take charge or take over, and when to step back. Live events need a subtle balance between process and competency, and everyone involved needs to rely on or have faith in leaders with relevant content or contextual experience.

With deadlines often immovable in any practical sense, the compression of time coupled with increased workloads leads to pressure that can manifest in different ways in different people. Understanding that even the simplest of tasks can, for some, become Herculean missions in particular circumstances, you will have greater compassion, and you or your team can be better prepared to deal with the effects of this pressure.

Change and chaos are inevitable, to think otherwise is short sighted, but this chaos can be quarantined with the right structure. There's no reason why you or your team need to be working in anything other than a calm and measured manner, despite what may be going on around you.

A central reference point – one set of plans and one schedule that everyone uses as their guide – is mandatory. These sets of plans and schedules work best if they exist in some shape or form from day one, the tipping point, to focus everyone's work, minds and discussions from the outset.

The insights I have shared in this chapter are subjective and difficult to measure. They are, though, the principles of the way I and those I work with operate. People who are led and supported empathetically are far more likely to go the extra mile to maximise an event's impact and deliver exceptional value.

Knowing what you need is one thing. How do you go about getting it, though?

6

Avoiding counterproductive paradoxes often created when the fluid nature of live events meets the typically non-fluid nature of procurement starts with insight.

Chapter 6

Procurement Paradox

Live events exist within a unique set of parameters, so finding or procuring the various things you need to bring them to fruition can be far from straightforward. Traditional techniques can often have unexpected results. The practices you think may or should find you the best value, most creative or most suitable solutions may not do. Foresight and relevant insight can help, though.

In this chapter we look at how to manage or accommodate a live event's unique parameters to derive better value, reduce risk, find the best ideas or creativity and increase the impact of your event, whether you're sourcing what you need from third parties or undertaking work within your own organisation.

Getting what you need

We've looked at what you need, now we need to look at how you go about getting it. I've split this into three chapters. This chapter contains vital insights, the next two chapters provide step-by-step guidelines for every requirement you will ever need, be that hiring personnel, outsourcing events in whole or in part, or buying or hiring equipment or services.

Getting what you need spans two areas of expertise: acquiring talent and acquiring goods and services, more commonly referred to as human resources and procurement. For simplicity, I use the term procurement in this book generally to mean the acquisition of anything, be it talent or goods and services.

I am neither a procurement professional nor a human resources professional. What I am is someone who has over twenty years' experience of wrestling with and guiding the procurement challenges of both the largest and smallest organisations in the world, and navigating human resources requirements for roles that are often hard to define. I have been the client and worked client-side, and I have been the agency/contractor (vendor) and worked agency/contractor side across almost every type of event. If you are a procurement or human resources professional, or have such resources available to you, the aim of the guidance in this and the next two chapters is to improve, support or augment your existing practices and knowledge with regard to live events rather than replace them.

The information in these three chapters is equally relevant for:

- Individuals, organisations or brands looking to build their own team and produce live events in house
- Individuals, organisations or brands looking to outsource the production of their live events in their entirety
- Individuals, organisations or brands looking to procure the

goods and services they need for the events they are producing in house

- Agencies or production companies looking to improve how they procure goods and services

Whether they're procuring or being procured, few people, I believe it's safe to say, relish the procurement process. I am also confident in saying that I have seen very few procurement exercises that do what they are supposed to do successfully: find the best or best value solution for a live event. This is no great surprise. Where does anyone turn in order to understand how live events work? How are live events best conceived, procured and produced?

There's very little guidance, and what guidance there is can be short sighted, focusing primarily on sector-specific issues rather than the live event itself. Alternatively, guidance can be skewed too heavily in the direction of one aspect of a live event – the content,

the price, or the process, to give just three examples – rather than the live event as a whole. Individuals, brands and organisations therefore adopt traditional or common procurement approaches that don't take into account two fundamental aspects of live events.

Firstly, it is almost impossible to define what it is you are procuring accurately at the procurement stage. Secondly, live events are typically fluid and evolving beasts. Procurement exercises, even with change control and variation procedures, are fairly rigid. As a result, live event procurement often becomes an exercise in compliance with the procurement process rather than one that's able to find the best value, ideas or solutions. Having to procure the expertise you need in order to work out what you need clearly creates a paradox.

How can you work out what expertise you need to procure for a live event before you have the expertise on board to work it out? Well, there are ways to do this, but they require insight and awareness.

Before we carry on, I need to cover two important issues that are common causes of confusion. Firstly, we need some clarity around the terminology I will use to describe talent, and then we need clarity around the terms I'll use to describe and talk about money.

Talent terminology

The terminology commonly used to define job titles and roles can be a real hindrance when you're trying to find the right people or put the right teams together, the main reason being that most terminology used to describe the roles people have in the world of live events is either abstract or so broad it is almost meaningless.

In the construction industry, everyone knows what an architect does, what the engineer does and what a builder does. In medicine, everyone knows what a doctor does, what a surgeon does and what a nurse does. In the film world, everyone – or the people who need to know, anyway – knows what a producer does and what a director does. Come to live events, though, and everything is far from clear.

Let's take the example of someone who leads a live event: the person responsible for driving it forward and making sure it happens. What would you call them? An account manager? A producer? Director? Event manager? Event planner? Project director?

Executive producer? CEO? Account director? Project manager? Depending on which sector you work in and/or your own experience, you'll likely pick one of these, or something else entirely. There is no standard terminology. Instead, the terminology varies wildly between sectors and the organisations within them, despite all live events having the same core structure.

One of the most abused words I've ever come across is the title that many people leading a live event, including me on occasions, assume, which is producer. This is, I am sure, a hangover from the theatrical and film worlds. I know producers who have little to no experience yet are considered to be on a level playing field with producers who have thirty years' experience. Why? It's because some people see a producer as the person at the top of the food chain, leading and directing things, while others see a producer as little more than a secretary with extra responsibilities. The title in itself means next to nothing. 'Producer' as a word has been used and abused so much that it's become almost meaningless. Unless you know the person taking on this title personally and are clearly aware of what it is they do, the title of producer doesn't help you to identify what they do at all.

When it comes to creative and content roles, the world of job titles becomes even more abstract. Creative director, content director, designer, experiential designer, experience designer, 3D designer, creative insight, strategy director, communications director, ideation expert, content producer, content director...the list is endless. From the job titles alone, it is almost impossible to fathom what functions the people with these titles undertake.

Once you drop beneath the management level, the titles and terminology become a little more sensible. Lighting designer, copywriter, stage manager, technical director, rigger, carpenter, designer, electrician, choreographer, venue manager, volunteer manager...these terms make sense. They speak for themselves.

But the terminology at a senior and management level is a problem, and as these are the roles that you will be looking for first, the problem needs addressing.

We have talked in detail about the four key roles you require to produce and deliver any live event: someone to lead things; someone to lead on the content; someone responsible for physically delivering everything; and someone to look after the operations and logistics. I deliberately didn't give these roles a title as I know the terminology would vary wildly by sector.

To illustrate my point, let's look at the typical terminology for three types of event: a sports event, an arts event and a business-to-business conference.

Sports event:

- Lead: event director
- Content: competition director/ sporting director
- Delivery: venue manager/site

manager/technical director/ overlay manager (or similar)

- Operations/logistics: operations manager

Arts event:

- Lead: producer/executive producer
- Content: artist/designer/creative director
- Delivery: production manager/ technical director (or similar)
- Operations: logistics manager/ operations manager (or similar)

Business-to-business conference:

- Lead: producer, account manager, event planner, event manager...the list is endless
- Content: producer, brand manager, creative director...again, the list is endless
- Delivery: production manager or director/technical director (or similar)
- Operations: logistics manager

As you can see, it's a mess. And imagine if an event involved all three of these sectors in one: sport plus art plus a brand's business-to-business activities.

At this point, you may be asking why this matters. It matters for two reasons. Firstly, you need to make sure you have the right people in the four key roles, and any other roles that you require subsequently. Secondly, focusing on titles isn't the best way of finding the right people. Unless you are looking for specific trades or disciplines, you are better off avoiding all terminology completely. Or if you do use terminology, make sure you explain what you mean by the role so it's clear. Most importantly, though, by no means can you assume that someone with a certain job title, either currently or previously, has what you need them to have to undertake a role with a similar title again. You may, for example, need a producer for a project. You may know a number of people with experience as producers, or people will come to you, citing their experience as a producer. Your version of what a producer does and theirs may be completely different, though.

Take an example of a mistake I once made. I was leading a live event, a ceremony, and I needed some films created. I knew exactly what I wanted; I just needed it filmed and edited.

I looked around and was really excited to find out that a well-known film maker was available to work on the film. His work was great, I could afford him, and so I snapped him up.

Things were going well until filming was about to start. The film maker knew a great deal about producing films, but very little about actually shooting them. Or to put it another way, we spent more time arguing about what I wanted in the film than anything else. He then had to get additional people involved to do the filming and editing. It became extremely difficult to get what I actually wanted, and cost a great deal more than it

needed to as I was paying for someone to do the work I'd already done.

As it turned out, I needed a director, not the film maker (who was actually a producer), or someone capable of being both a producer and director, to bring the film I had already conceived and mapped out to life. We all live and learn.

This example highlights the problems that come from focusing too much on job titles, although admittedly, my lack of knowledge at the time did play a part, too.

Unless you know exactly what you are looking for and what people have done before, it is best to avoid job titles and terminology completely, or at least, don't rely on them. Instead, simply detail in straightforward layman's terms what you expect each person you get on board to do and, sometimes more importantly, what you don't expect them to do.

Budgets, quotes, costs and estimates

Four of the most confused words when it comes to live events are:

- Budget
- Quote
- Cost
- Estimate

A **budget** is a lump of money you make available. It's a target or limit. The event's budget is not the cost of an event.

A **quote** is a number: a price a supplier gives either in return for a specification or their interpretation of a brief. A quote is not a budget. A quote is also not necessarily the final cost or price of the specification or scope.

The **cost** of an event, or part of an event, is what the event or element of an event costs. In all but the rarest of occasions, it is impossible to know what the final cost of an event will be until the event has happened. Until then, there is no such thing as a cost of an event; there is merely an estimate.

An **estimate** is exactly that: an estimate, or best guess as I like to call it, ideally backed up with experience.

Before we look at each of these in turn, remember the circumstances in which live events usually exist:

- You have continually changing or evolving specifications
- You have a deadline that can't move
- You're completely exposed; everyone is watching
- You, or those you bring on board, are rarely in control of everything affecting your success

Budget. Unless you are in complete control of everything and know everything, it's impossible to know what an event will cost. However, creating a budget that covers everything and protects you against all reasonable eventualities is relatively straightforward, provided the people doing so have the right content and contextual experience.

If you find yourself basing your budget on quotes you've received for briefs that are open to interpretation, which is almost every brief, you need to make sure that either you have the expertise to manage such a project personally and protect your budget, or you must assume that any quote is going to rise. It may not, but you don't know this at the early budgeting stage of an event.

Quote. If you're asking for a quote, maybe from a supplier, an agency, or a contractor, this quote will be based on what you ask them to quote for. But it's unlikely that whatever you're asking for a quote on will remain the same between the quote stage and the event happening. There are so many variables at play, some within your control and some beyond your control.

Do not regard any quote you receive as a cost; it's merely a quote upon which to base your budget. Someone with relevant content and contextual experience will need to make a judgment call on whether any quote is realistic, and whether to accept the quote and work with whomever provided it to make sure the cost ends up being the same as the quote, or allow some additional funds within the budget on top of the quote as a contingency for the changes and additions that are inevitable.

Time and time again, I see people asking for a quote to be a fixed cost for something. Unless you are providing a highly detailed specification, for example 'Ten lights of type xyz' or 'Three days of xyz work', a fixed cost is never going to be a fixed cost. A quote may come back looking like a fixed cost, but it will be accompanied by so many caveats (exclusions) that it is merely a guide.

Consider, too, that even if you receive and accept a quote as a fixed cost, as the live event evolves and the parameters change, the person, supplier or agency you're dealing with may end up facing increased pressures in trying to honour the quote. If you take a pure, cold-hearted contractual approach, you may see this as the supplier's problem. However, given the speed at which live events move and the fact you have a deadline that can't move, if a supplier or agency fails or lets you down in any way, the problem that was (and is) theirs contractually quickly becomes yours in reality. No contract is worth the paper it's printed on at the moment you're about to go live. There needs to be some give and take, some flexibility on both sides of any contract as parameters change.

It is, of course, possible to ask a supplier or agency to include realistic contingencies within their quote. In fact, this is normal and common. Then the quote is not really a quote; it's merely a budget (or a portion of a budget) that someone is managing on your behalf.

Cost. The cost of an item or service is the final cost: the amount in pounds, dollars or any other currency that actually leaves your bank account.

When you're looking at quotes, the cost of something will only match the quote if nothing changes. If you're getting quotes on unit costs, these needn't change and should be fixed, assuming no parameters surrounding those units or their use change. However, if you're getting quotes for turnkey solutions, products, a whole event or similar, things will change. You won't know the final cost until you have completed the event. No one does.

Estimate. Everything money-wise involved with a live event is essentially an estimate until the event has happened. The budget is an estimate, quotes are largely estimates, and no one knows the actual cost until you're done, so if you hear anyone using the word 'cost' for anything other than a specific, quantifiable unit of something, they mean an estimate. It's safest to see a figure as an estimate at all times.

A public screening event I was involved with is a great example to illustrate what I mean here. This event was to be held in a big public space where people would gather to watch live activities on a large outdoor screen.

The client who wanted the screening had the idea, and then asked around colleagues and associates what they thought such an event may cost. The client got back examples of similar events and the budgets that various people had spent, or thought they had spent, on them. The client then formed an opinion in their mind of what the event was going to cost based on these responses.

Wanting a little more certainty before committing, the client put some tenders out to discover what the equipment they needed may cost. As they were simply asking for equipment costs without knowing where the event was going to be or resolving a myriad of other contextual issues, the quotes that came back were covered in caveats. However, they did look similar to the costs the client had received from their initial research, asking colleagues and associates.

This client didn't have any contextual experience. Why would they? Producing and delivering live events wasn't their normal function, so they were merely relying on the information they'd received.

Now happy to proceed, but wanting to offset the risk and have someone manage everything for them, the client put out a new tender for a turnkey solution to produce the event and supply all the equipment. By this time, the client had chosen a location for the event, but that, along with the event's date, was the only definite information they could supply. Naturally, everyone who wanted to submit a response to the tender had numerous questions they needed answering in order to provide an accurate, or even reasonable, quote. This being a competitive situation, no one responding to the tender was going to suggest that things may cost more than they needed to.

Eventually, the client awarded the tender. It was a fixed price contract, but had within it contingencies the client thought would be enough to cover all and any unknowns.

It was only at this point that planning started in earnest. The client had already announced that the event would take place on their chosen date, so cancelling or postponing it wasn't really an option. But within days of the planning starting, a whole host of issues arose: everything from the owners of the venue having fixed views on where the client could position the screen through to restrictions on what advertising they could display on the screens. There were a myriad of other issues, too, but the position of the screen alone meant that the client required a much larger screen, which inevitably had a significant effect on the budget. The advertising restrictions at the location meant that the adverts in the commercial breaks of the broadcast needed replacing locally with additional content that had to be created – yet more pressure on the budget. This then led to conversations about who was at fault – who should bear this additional cost? Was it the client because the specification had effectively changed, or was it the agency that had agreed to deliver the project on a quote it had provided based on loose scope from the client?

The legally correct response to this would lie in the detail. However, if you were to detail everything you may need for a live event down to the last nut and bolt, you would spend more time drafting contracts than producing or delivering the event. This inevitably makes details vague on both sides of the contract, which is why relationships and competence matter as much as contracts and due diligence.

Consider, too, that if both sides were going to rectify the situation in my example with legally correct due diligence, it wouldn't have been resolved until long after the event was due to happen.

In this scenario, the client didn't know the true scope and specification of the event until well into the planning. But they couldn't start the planning until after they had awarded the tender to the people who would do the planning, and rather than just find people who could help, they decided to find a full turnkey solution – the help they needed and the equipment. The true problem here was how the client tendered the event out in the first place. Although this is an extremely common way of tendering out live events, it's not necessarily the best way, as we'll go on to explore.

In the end, the situation resolved itself with the client finding a little more money and the agency involved juggling some activity around, but the amount of time both sides had spent on sorting the issue out was considerable – all time that the client, whether they realised it or not, would end up paying for, either in cash or through elements of their event being compromised. The client went through considerable stress, too, worrying about their supplier potentially letting them down and the embarrassment and risk of having to find more money.

One could argue that the client in this instance should, to an extent, have been able to rely on the competence of the people they had brought on board to offer the right advice. However, when a client's procurement process either doesn't allow the scope for such advice, or creates a conflict of interest for the supplier between offering what the client's asked for in a way that makes them competitive and telling the client everything they need to hear, even if they may not want to hear it, which would make the supplier less competitive or attractive, therein lies an extremely common problem.

Here we have an example of a client firstly creating an unrealistic budget without the relevant contextual experience. Then they received a quote which they believed to be fixed and quickly discovering it wasn't. The costly lesson the client learned was that the final cost of the event wouldn't become known until the project was completed. Until that point, everything was merely an estimate.

All of the issues in this example are easy to sort out as part of the development and planning process, yet they continue to make a mockery of many people's procurement processes. There are ways to find the right company and ensure you get the best value, even when you know all too well that your plans may change.

Budget contingency

If you're embarking on anything live, please use this reminder as guidance:

- A **budget** is merely an allocation of money assigned to cover a requirement
- A **quote** is a figure you receive against a specification. This quote will change if the specification does, and probability wise, it will
- A **cost** is what an event or part of an event finally costs, which you will rarely know with absolute assurance until after the event, unless the event is straightforward or formulaic. Unit costs can be fixed, but the costs for turnkey or packaged solutions can't be unless the supplier takes on the risk of parameters changing, which will become your risk again if the supplier faces issues trying to stick to a fixed budget as the requirements change, or become clearer
- An **estimate** is exactly that: an estimate. Treat any quote or cost you get pre-event as an estimate

This sounds like a recipe for disaster. How can you manage a budget if everything is always an estimate? The answer is to have relevant contextual and content experts on board to make and manage a budget contingency. People with contextual and content experience, involved at the right time, will know, or be able to work out, what similar activity has cost previously, and they'll recognise which costs can be pinned down immediately and how much may come out of the woodwork as plans evolve. With this knowledge, your experts can then help you to allow sufficient contingency within a budget, proportional to the scale, level of completeness and complexity of the activity you're embarking on.

One important note about contingency: the quickest way to make sure a contingency fund will get used is to declare that there is a contingency fund. It is best to deny all knowledge of a contingency fund: don't tell anyone it exists; don't discuss it with anyone involved in spending your budgets or developing the requirements the budgets need to cover. This might be tricky to carry out to the letter, so use your discretion. Only use or commit funds from any contingency budget when those

with relevant content or contextual experience confirm either that there won't be any more demands on the contingency plan or what reduced contingency plans you still need to hold.

Who's paying?

There are essentially only two fundamentally different ways in which events are funded. If you are an individual or organisation looking to use your money, or money you've raised or plan to raise, you will be funding your own team and any suppliers, or you'll be outsourcing everything to a third party. It's plain and simple.

We'll call this option the funded approach. The live event has funding in place, or at least a plan to acquire the funds.

If you don't plan on funding the event yourself, you'll be looking for someone else to pay for things (or some things). If you have certain rights or benefits you can offer, you may be able to find someone to take those rights or benefits, profit from them, and in return deliver your event for you in its entirety or at a reduced cost to you.

For example, the International Olympic Committee (IOC) awards the rights to host the Olympic Games to a city. That city takes the rights, sells tickets, sells on various rights, raises sponsorship, and uses the money it gains as a result (and any other funding) to deliver the Games. The IOC gets the Games it wants, and the city benefits from the impact the Games bring.

The owner of an iconic location or venue may recognise the value of their plot of land during a particular season, for example Christmas. They may then award the exclusive rights to use that land to a promoter in return for a fee, commission or both. The promoter may stage a Christmas fair, profiting from the opportunity themselves, and the landowner gets the marketing benefits of the fair and the fees from the promoter.

Maybe you want to stage a high-profile event, for example the opening of a new building, a major celebration, or a global expo or summit. Given the attention such an event is likely to receive, you may consider awarding the rights to profit from the event to a promoter. They would sell tickets and raise sponsorship or fundraise to deliver the event for you and make a profit for themselves.

We'll call this option the promoter approach.

I'm using the generic term 'promoter' here to mean a person or organisation capable of securing the funding, sponsorship, customers or audience for an event. It may well be an event agency, or someone who has an event team. An event agency or event company may or may not have the ability to be a promoter, as this uses a different skillset: selling and sales as opposed to producing and delivery. Likewise, you need to check any promoter has the ability to develop, produce and deliver an event, too, either on their own or in partnership with an event organisation. I will provide details of how to find and/or contract whatever you need in the next two chapters.

The funded and promoter approaches carry different risks. But although they're extremely different, the two approaches can be combined. For example, if you run an organisation that wishes to stage a large conference or exhibition, you may need, or choose, to adopt the funded approach to fund the team (be that in house or outsourced) to produce, design and develop the event, yet also need the team to adopt the promoter approach to sell exhibition space and sponsorship packages to offset all or some of the costs you're underwriting.

If you don't have an obvious set of rights or benefits to offer, the promoter route can be extremely high risk. If your live event simply has to happen and be delivered without fail, and it can't be cancelled or postponed, then relying on a promoter to sell tickets and find sponsorship or funding in some way leaves you exposed to considerable risk. If that promoter fails to find sponsorship or funding, you're likely to end up in trouble or liable for the costs yourself. No contract guaranteeing fundraising, sponsorship or ticket sales is going to help you if the promoter simply doesn't have the funds, and the problem will be back on your desk very quickly. You therefore need to think carefully about choosing the promoter route if your live event isn't an established event or one with a proven revenue stream or commercial interest in its associated rights or benefits.

In summary, you're either paying for an event yourself, the funded approach, or you need to find a promoter who'll take the rights to the benefits you can offer in return for the event you want or need. And if you're offering rights and benefits, you need to be sure those rights and benefits have the commercial value you think they have before committing to the event.

Value in kind

I want to talk briefly about value in kind (VIK), which is when you receive some type of value at zero financial cost in return for benefits such as sponsorship or association.

For example, an airline may provide flights for free to event participants or staff in return for branding opportunities and other rights at an event. A technical supplier may provide equipment for an event in return for branding and association rights. A venue or service provider may offer their venue or service for free or at a greatly reduced rate if the event benefits an objective or strategy of theirs, or in return for brand exposure or marketing rights. Almost anything can theoretically be offered as VIK.

While it's not relevant or applicable to all events, VIK can be a huge benefit. You shouldn't snap up VIK offers without applying the same due diligence as you would to a contract you'd be paying money for, though. It can be tempting to grab all and any VIK deals – after all, who doesn't love free stuff? But free doesn't always mean good value. Free items or services may end up costing you a great deal more to secure or work with than it would have cost to purchase them at standard commercial rates.

You need to make a value judgment. If someone offers you some technical equipment that may save you, say, $10,000 at face value, it would seem like a great deal. If, however, it's going to cost you $3,000 in people's time to secure the deal, $3,000 to have the equipment collected and delivered back again, and $5,000 to have the equipment modified and made ready for the event, then its value diminishes rapidly if you could have been secured the same turnkey solution for $10,000 yourself. This is a common situation: people deal with VIK offers often, but few focus on the comparative value calculation.

Consider, too, that if a company is providing something as VIK, the level of service you will get may change, as may the balance of power. Whereas a contractor/client relationship, a standard commercial arrangement, will typically see the contractor bend over backwards to support you as the client, when the contractor is supplying its services as VIK, they can hold or feel like they hold the upper hand and the service can sometimes be less forthcoming.

Consider, too, whether what you're being offered is actually good value. A VIK deal from a hotel chain that offers free rooms for attendees at an event in return for prime positioning as a sponsor can seem like a great deal. But if the rooms the hotel is offering equate to, say, £500/night, yet you could get equivalent hotel rooms by paying £250/night in cash at another hotel, the deal you are getting is far from good value. You could do two deals for the same in-kind value if you analyse it in detail.

I always advise people and organisations to get comparative quotes and offers for goods and services at a supplier's best commercial price. Once you have a competitive price, you will know the value of the services a supplier can offer, and can then start discussing or considering offers for VIK, assured that you are getting good value.

Summary

If the right core team in the right place at the right time is the most important thing when you're producing and delivering a live event, how you procure or appoint your teams, along with how you or they procure the goods and services you need to support a live event, is the second most important thing. The two go hand in hand.

It is extremely common for people to apply traditional or typical procurement approaches and practices to the world of live events. So much of my professional life is spent trying to unpick or reverse-engineer issues that have arisen because of the manner in which goods or services or turnkey solutions have been procured. The waste of time, money and effort, along with the frustration that well-intentioned yet flawed procurement exercises cause, is considerable. With some simple changes, though, you can avoid much of this waste and anxiety.

In this chapter, we have also looked at some of the traditional job titles that can cause confusion when you're looking for talent to lead your live event. Your definition of a producer, for example, may be completely different to that of the person applying to take on the role, so rather than relying on job titles, you'll be far more successful in getting the right people into the right places at the right time if you describe exactly what you expect, in layman's terms, from them during the procurement stage.

We then had a look at four consistently misunderstood words: budget, quote, cost and estimate. If you're embarking on anything live, please use the following guidance:

- A **budget** is merely an allocation of money assigned to cover a requirement
- A **quote** is a figure you receive against a specification; this quote will change if the specification does, and in all probability, it will
- A **cost** (or price) is what an event or part of an event finally costs, which you will rarely know with

absolute assurance until after the event, unless the event is straightforward or formulaic; unit costs can be fixed, but the costs for turnkey or packaged solutions can't be unless the supplier takes on the risk of parameters changing, which will become your risk again if the supplier faces issues that hold work up

- An **estimate** is exactly that: an estimate; treat any quote or cost you get pre-event as an estimate

How can you manage a budget when the ever-evolving nature of a live event means that you won't know the costs until after it has taken place? The answer is to have the right contextual and content experts in place from the outset as they will be able to predict the potential risks and ensure there is sufficient well-managed contingency in place.

We then covered who will actually be paying for the event. Will you be funding it or raising the funds yourself – the funded approach – or do you have rights and benefits you can sell on to a promoter in return for them producing and delivering the event you require – the promoter approach? If you're offering rights and benefits to a promoter, you need to be sure those rights and benefits have the commercial value you think they have before committing to the event.

Finally, we covered VIK, which can seem like a win/win for both you and your suppliers. However, you need to dig deeper to ensure that what the supplier is offering does indeed represent good value, or could you actually procure the same goods or services for less than the cost of the extra work the VIK offer will entail?

All live events share more similarities than differences structurally. They all exist in a unique set of circumstances, and many events consist of different types of events in one, for example sports events that also involve entertainment and exhibitions. Given all these similarities, we need more effective approaches to procuring goods, services and talent. Over the years, I have developed and refined procurement processes that are proven to work. They focus on three key objectives: creating the maximum impact, deriving the best value or return possible, and minimising risks.

Over the next two chapters, I will share these processes with you.

7

A powerful toolkit to get you what your live event needs, when you need it, even if you don't know exactly what you need.

Chapter 7

Procurement Toolkit Part 1: Overview, Goods And Services

First we provide an overview of the whole procurement toolkit, detailing the only six approaches necessary to get anything you will ever need for a live event or to outsource a live event in its entirety, even if you don't know exactly what you need, but know you need something. This simple yet powerful procurement toolkit works for anything.

We then focus the first three of these six approaches: how to best procure the goods and services necessary for a live event, no matter how small or gargantuan, no matter how common, niche or completely bespoke.

Everything you need for a live event falls into one of two categories, goods or services: equipment, temporary or permanent buildings, technology, scenery, plants, flowers, tradespeople, emergency services, professional services, staff, crew, artists, animals, weaponry, vehicles – and everything and anything in between.

Armed with the important insights in this chapter, we then go on to explore procuring turnkey solutions in the second part of the procurement toolkit, in the next chapter.

Live event procurement toolkit

Live events can necessitate the need for any imaginable 'thing' or amount of 'stuff' under the sun: equipment, temporary or permanent buildings, technology, scenery, plants, flowers, tradespeople, emergency services, professional services, military, staff, crew, artists, animals, weaponry, vehicles... anything.

To make your life a little simpler, I have designed a simple live event procurement toolkit and divided it into sections to make the information easily navigable. When you understand this toolkit fully, you will be well prepared for any eventuality or requirement. You can, of course, use the toolkit's different approaches in combination or at different stages of any live event. You can also find a quick reference guide at www.TheFactsOfLive.com

There are only ever going to be three types of things you need for a live event: goods, services or a turnkey solution. I don't want to get too hung up on terminology as it can vary wildly, even between people in the same company doing the same thing. In summary, though:

Goods are physical units of stuff either off the shelf or that need manufacturing. If the goods you require fall into the second category, you will also need to take into account the resources and labour to manufacture and deliver the goods.

In terms of live event procurement, the term goods can cover anything that could be perceived as a commodity, for example:

- Technical equipment
- Scenery, props, dressing and staging
- Branding
- Venue or location hire
- Temporary architecture and structures
- New buildings, construction and landscaping
- Furniture
- Catering

- Plant and machinery
- Non-specialist labour
- Security

It may seem odd to include labour and security as examples of goods. While these are arguably services rather than goods, they are procured as commodities. Typically, you procure labour and security by specifying the type and quantity you require, so they fall into the goods category when it comes to procurement. Knowing or working out what labour is needed or developing a security or stewarding plan, for example, is specialist knowledge or professional expertise, and is covered below under services.

Services are people and support, be it expertise, systems or manpower. Examples of services include:

- Producers, event directors/ managers, project managers and similar
- Event professionals with any title
- Designers and creatives

- Talent, artists and performers
- Accountants and lawyers
- Lighting, sound and video designers
- Film, software and digital specialists
- Technology expertise
- Marketing, PR, advertising, sponsorship and commercial expertise
- Ticketing and accreditation expertise
- Security, stewarding, volunteer marshals, traffic and transport specialists

Turnkey solutions are a combination of both goods and services, for example:

- An event agency that will produce, design, and then physically deliver a live event (or part of one)
- A production company that will take your idea or concept and provide the resources and equipment to deliver it

- A promoter who will sell your event rights, tickets or other assets in return for delivering your event at no or a reduced cost
- An artist or designer who will develop an exhibit, installation or piece of art for an event and then create or deliver it

If you can't currently work out whether what you need would be classified as goods, services or a turnkey solution, it may well become clear as you read through the ways I suggest to procure each category.

Check what you need

The simple procurement toolkit consists of the only six approaches you'll ever need:

1. Procuring goods with a specification: you know exactly what you want and can specify your requirements accurately

2. Procuring goods without a specification: you know what you need but you can't yet specify your requirements accurately

3. Procuring services: you have identified the professional services, expertise or talent that you need for your event

4. Procuring a flexible turnkey solution: you know you want a turnkey solution and either don't yet know what shape your live event will take or know that it will change between brief and delivery

5. Procuring a fixed turnkey solution: you're looking for a turnkey solution and your requirements will not change, regardless of the decisions you make or of external forces or circumstances between brief and delivery – which is extremely rare

6. Procuring or finding a promoter: you intend to sell the rights for your event to a promoter to sell on and deliver your event at less or no cost to you, in line with agreed terms.

The simple flowchart, the tipping point choices depicted in Figure 7.1, will help you check what approach you need at any given time. Whether you know what you need, think you know what you need, or don't know what you need at all, it is worth going through this flowchart a few times to be sure.

Do you have, or think you have, rights or benefits you can offer that are of value? If you do, then you may consider looking for a promoter to effectively take the rights to your event, exploit them commercially and deliver your event in return; at no or less cost to you. Make sure, though, that you understand the realistic value of any rights or benefits you have to offer, and in turn what you may have to give up in order for those rights to be exploited (to become profitable). For example, if you own a brand and want an event to launch or promote it, you may have to have other brands displayed prominently at the event, you may have less control over your event, and you may have less control over who attends.

If your event is critical in so far as it has to happen, you will need to be certain the rights you have to offer have enough value to cover the costs you hope they will. If you, or the promoter you bring on board, fail to sell the rights or the tickets or raise enough money, your event will be at risk. You can ask for contractual guarantees or for the promoter to underwrite the cost of the event, but even with a contract in place, if the promoter fails, it is unlikely there will be enough time to rectify the situation satisfactorily before the event is due to go ahead (unless you build in key milestones), making the

problem, and risk, very much yours. Generally speaking, unless your event has proven commercial revenue streams or a number of qualified independent people have confirmed your event will make the money you think it will, your rights probably won't have the value you think they do. You will only know, though, by testing the market.

A more common approach, without such rights, will see you funding everything yourself with your own money or money you've raised, or plan to raise, yourself (or have others raise for you) by selling sponsorship, tickets or whatever else. For this approach, you have two options.

Firstly you can find an organisation, agency or company to provide you with a turnkey solution – all the people (services) and goods to develop and deliver your live event. This isn't your only option, though. Maybe you want to do things yourself or with your own team. But is your team in place? If

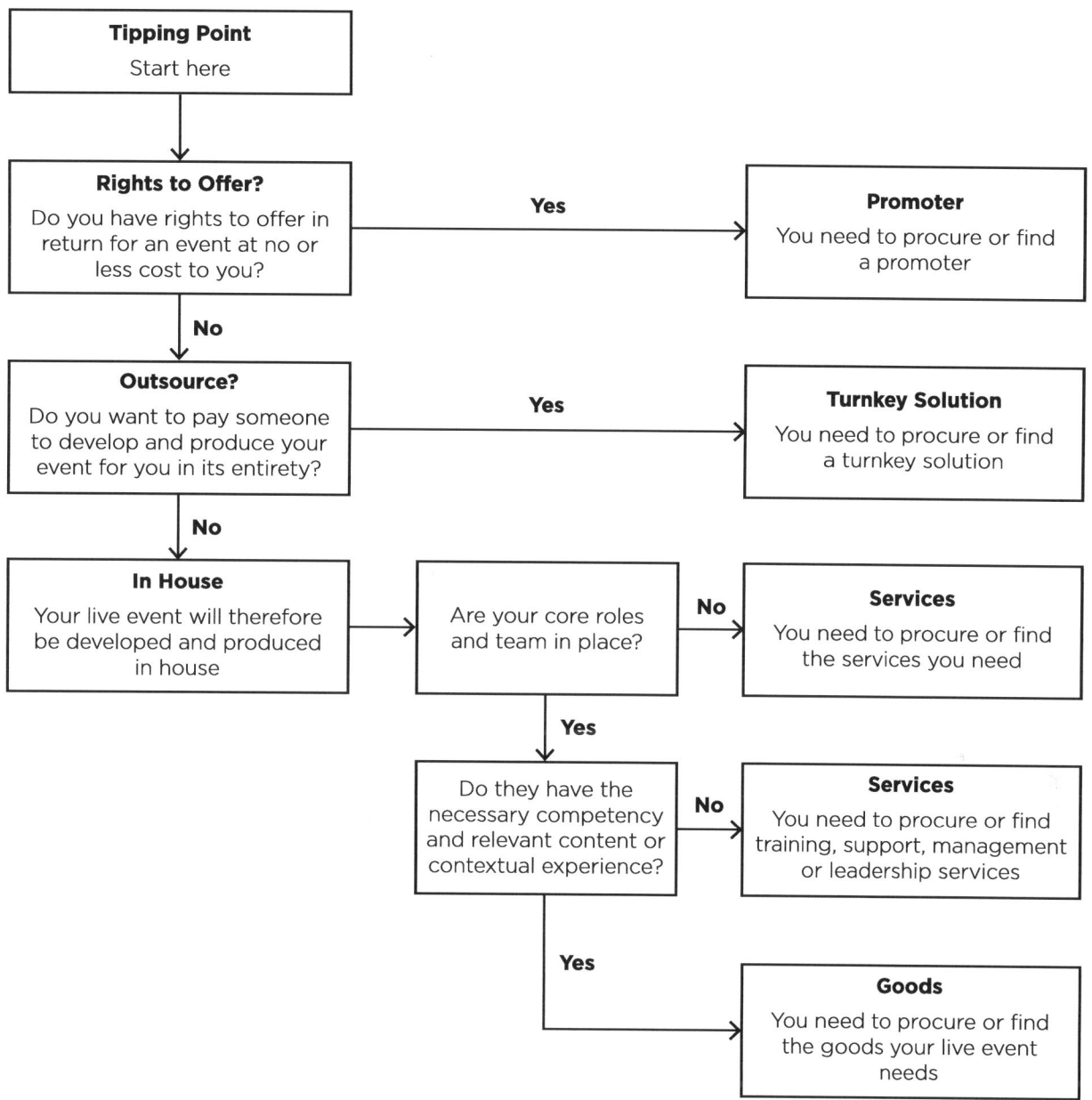

Figure 7.1: Tipping point choices

it isn't, you're going to need to find the right people (services). If it is, do the people on your team have the relevant content and contextual experience? If they don't, they are going to need some training or support (services). If they do have the relevant experience, you, or they, are good to start developing and planning your live event. All you will need to do is outsource the goods once your plans have evolved.

In reality, a more complex event may require a combination of turnkey solutions, goods and services, but it's still fairly simple to work out what you need. All you need to do is take each aspect of a live event through the flowchart in Figure 7.1.

Let's look at some different examples.

- **Producing an event in house.** You work for a brand that wants to build an internal team to produce its own conferences, product launches, exhibitions or other live events. First, you will need to find the person or people who will undertake the four key roles we identified in the previous chapters. In this case, you are looking for services and will follow the correct approach to find the services you need.

Once the team is on board and up to speed, as the designs and plans develop, you and your team will approach the point of needing to deliver the event. This requires goods, so you will follow one of these approaches to secure the goods you need.

- **An established event with proven sponsorship and ticketing revenue streams.** If you want to sell the sponsorship and tickets for your event yourself or with an organisation you're involved with, you will be either producing the event yourself with a team you already have, finding the services you need, or outsourcing the requirement using one of the turnkey approaches.

- **Outsourcing to a company to design, produce and deliver an event that also needs sponsorship packages and tickets to be sold.** Firstly, you need to find the company to design, produce and deliver the event. You need a turnkey solution, so follow one of the approaches to secure that solution.

  You, your team, or the turnkey solution provider will then need to sell sponsorship packages and tickets for the event. You have a choice here. You can either find one company that can do all of this as part of the turnkey solution, whether the company does all the work itself or outsources (subcontracts) some of the work, or you can outsource this to a specialist promoter as a separate contract or contracts. If you choose to find one company to produce the event and promote it (sell rights, tickets and anything else that can be sold), you will simply need to combine one of the turnkey solution approaches with the promoter approach.

- **An arts festival.** If you represent an organisation that wants to produce or commission an arts festival, you first need to find the team that will produce it. You have a couple of options.

  You could build an in-house team that will lead, produce and curate the festival by following the services approach. As the festival evolves, different performances, artists and acts would then be sourced on a case-by-case basis. Events could be outsourced as turnkey solutions and solo performances as services.

  Alternatively, you could outsource the entire festival to one lead organisation as a turnkey solution. You then just need to check how the organisation you choose will, in turn, outsource or contract the various requirements of the festival before you appoint it. You have the guidance and approaches in this book to help you assess or compare how each organisation you look at will operate on your behalf.

- **Event agency looking for improvements.** If you represent an event agency, production company or similar looking to improve your approach to procurement, you can combine your own experience to date with the procurement approaches and guidance throughout this book to secure the goods and services you and/or your clients require. If you are producing or managing a larger, more complex event, you can adopt the turnkey solutions for sub-events or discrete areas of activity to improve how you find the partners you want to work with.

As you can see, there are a number of ways you can combine or use the six approaches in the live event procurement toolkit as and when you need them.

These are the only approaches you will ever need to get anything you require to produce and deliver a live event. A quick reference guide summarising all six approaches can be found at www.TheFactsOfLive.com

Now let's look at the first three of the six procurement approaches in the toolkit: the ones dealing with goods and services.

Procuring goods with a specification

If you know exactly what you want, you have expertise with a certain type of goods, you know that nothing is going to change and you can accurately specify what you need, you're good to go. Let's check this theory, though. A specification should be a specification and not merely an idea or indication.

For example, if you were looking for some lights for an event, this would be a specification (or part of one): 'ETC Source 4 Lantern 750W'.

The specification details the make and model of the lamp. Add in how many you need along with the associated equipment and you have yourself a specification for a lighting rig.

This, however, isn't a specification: 'Lighting rig for a stage performance'. This is a scope, or brief. It is open to interpretation and still needs someone to do some work on it to create a specification.

This is a simple example, but unless you have the necessary expertise, your 'specification' may well be open to interpretation, like the second example above. In that case, you're not going to be comparing like for like when you're looking for parity between suppliers.

If you do know how to specify your requirements, or have someone on your team who does, great. If you don't, you can do one of two things. You can seek out the expertise you need, which we're coming to shortly, before procuring the goods, or you can follow the approach I provide to secure the goods you need without a specification.

Other examples of what are and aren't specifications:

- This is a specification: '10 x security guards of type xyz for eight hours to perform tasks abc'
- This isn't a specification: 'Appropriate security for the event' (this is a brief; it is open to interpretation)
- This is a specification: 'A piece of scenery accompanied by a full set

of construction drawings, finishes and specifications for its use, with details of when it's needed, access and location'

- This isn't a specification: 'A piece of scenery with some visual references and mood images' (this is a brief; it is open to interpretation)

Assuming you can accurately specify your requirements to a level that is unambiguous to the companies you'll be sending the specification to, there are six steps to take to procure goods with a specification.

1. Specify the goods you need, when and where you need them, for what duration, and any other relevant requirements. Add any goods-specific guidance or clarifications necessary.

For example, electrical equipment may need certain safeguards or if you're looking for a venue, you will need to specify all relevant contractual requirements you have. This is why you and/or your team need the relevant expertise to specify the goods and associated information correctly. Add any governance requirements if you need or want to, for example, health and safety checks, environmental checks, financial standing, sustainability management, quality assurance checks etc, or any other criteria important to you and/ or appropriate to the size and type of the event. Importantly, make sure you ask for prices, too. It sounds obvious, but I have seen tenders, requests and briefs sent out without any price requests.

2. Distribute your specification of requirements in whatever way works for you or your organisation to a relevant supplier, or suppliers if you want to compare prices for an identical specification.

3. Assess the responses you receive on the quality and value of the goods you're looking for. Look closely at any caveats, notes or exclusions. Conduct interviews or clarifications if they're necessary.

4. Check references relevant to the goods you're looking for if you're not familiar with the suppliers who are responding. Perform any governance checks you deem necessary.

5. Appointment. Agree the price or unit prices and confirm your requirements.

6. Management. Don't assume that once you've confirmed your requirements or ordered your goods, they will just turn up. Keep in close contact with your suppliers to check they have what they need and are fully informed of what you expect from them. Ideally, they will become deeply involved with the planning process if you set up a two-way liaison throughout the project.

Some would argue that once you have procured and ordered the goods you need, the job is done. If you didn't have an immovable deadline, this may be an acceptable approach. For a live event, though, continuous liaison and support between you or your team and your suppliers should be the norm. Keep in mind that events evolve. It is highly likely that any requirements you agree with your suppliers will change, so keep arrangements flexible where you can. Without this type of relationship, you won't know everything is OK, you will only think you know. As the event nears, no amount of paperwork or agreements can help you if a supplier has misunderstood something or you've miscommunicated something, so ensure any suppliers are supported and supervised, both before the event and once they're on site.

Procuring goods without a specification

If you, or your team, know you need certain goods, infrastructure, manufacturing, contractors or suppliers, but you either don't know how to specify them, or don't yet know exactly what you need, you will likely want the help and support of those who can supply the goods in order to develop a plan or specification. This is a common scenario and an approach that works extremely well.

Even if you think you know what you want, events change, so whatever you think you need now has a high likelihood of changing. You can hope it won't, but it's far better to assume that it will.

Maybe you know you need a lighting rig, but have no clue how to design one. Maybe you need some software to manage registration, but what solution is best? Maybe you need some scenery, but who can design it based on your sketches or ideas? Maybe you need security, but is what you really want a security firm to develop a plan for you before you, or they, can specify what security you actually need? You must make sure that you select a contractor capable of giving you the best advice and support to get the best value as plans evolve while ensuring you're not going to get ripped off.

While there is time to change suppliers, the power lies with you as the client. As the event date approaches, it becomes increasingly difficult to change supplier, and then the balance of power shifts from client to supplier. Your deadline isn't likely to move, the suppliers are embedded in the management team, design or planning process, and the availability of equipment or manufacturing times may also factor into the equation. At this point, you need the supplier more than the supplier needs you. It's important to be aware of this. It's unlikely to ever be articulated, but it's a subtle yet important nuance.

This may sound complicated or fraught, yet the solution to procuring goods without a specification is straightforward if you follow these six simple guidelines.

1. Brief. Write a brief, detailing what types of goods you're looking for and the likely location, date, type and scale of the event. If you don't know the details yet, estimate as much as possible and indicate that the details may change. It's much easier for a supplier if they have at least some idea of the scope and scale of the event.

Explain you're looking for a supplier to work with you to develop the specification and provide the goods you need. Use plain English; avoid acronyms or industry-specific jargon wherever possible.

Ask the suppliers only to detail unit costs of typical or example goods so you can compare their value like for like (a parity check) if it's equipment you are looking for. Be explicit; literally say, 'This exercise is a parity check between suppliers to find the best value goods. Once we've found a supplier we want to work with, we will develop the final specification with their support and expertise.' This saves suppliers trying to second guess what you're doing.

For example, if you're looking for a security firm to provide security and stewards, simply ask for their rates. Give some indication of whether you are likely to need tens or hundreds of security personnel, even if it's only a rough estimate. It helps if the suppliers you're approaching know what your likely requirements will be, and a brief overview of the event will give them enough context to work with.

Unit costs are straightforward when you're buying commodities like security personnel or technical equipment. When you're buying goods that require manufacturing or are less quantifiable, for example scenery, props, bespoke furniture and specialised technical equipment, asking for unit costs clearly won't be possible. You can, however, agree key milestones and payment terms.

In this instance, you are going to be comparing track records, the suppliers' experience, references, their approach and suggestions, and the chemistry you have with them. Ask if they have the capacity to supply or create your likely requirements, again providing them with a brief outline of the event. There's nothing else you can assess in any meaningful, quantifiable terms.

Finally, all goods are not equal and all suppliers are not the same. Allow suppliers to point out things they think are important for you to consider above and beyond any parity check. There may be a good reason why they don't feel they are able to respond exactly in the way you've asked, and it may help you. If you feel the things they suggest are irrelevant, you can ignore them, but rather than get strict about it, allow suppliers the opportunity to add anything they think is relevant and ask you questions.

Again, you can add any governance requirements if you need or want to.

2. Distribute your brief in whatever way works for you or your organisation to suppliers you believe can support you.

3. Assess the responses you receive on the quality and value of the goods you're looking for. Look closely at any caveats, notes or exclusions. Conduct interviews or clarifications if they're necessary. You'll be working closely with this supplier, as if they are one of your own team, so chemistry is important, too.

Assuming the responses come back using the same terminology as each other, you will know how the suppliers measure up financially and value-wise against each other. If the responses come back using terminology you don't understand or that's different on each response, simply ask each supplier to use the same terminology. Be explicit: say you're comparing responses and that's why you need comparable information.

4. Check references relevant to the goods you're looking for if you're not familiar with the suppliers who are responding. Perform any governance checks you deem necessary.

If need be, ask the suppliers to send you examples of their work, and ask them to make clear what their specific part of the project was. If you're given generic terms or it sounds like they did everything (few companies ever do everything on any given event), ask them to be more specific. Then do the 'content and context' test. If you are looking for help from a supplier to guide the content or purpose of your event, then they will need relevant content experience. If you are looking for help delivering or facilitating your event, the supplier will need relevant contextual experience of events with similar scale, complexity, budgets, types of location and, if applicable, marketing and commercial activity.

If you don't have the experience to guide your suppliers, they will need to have the experience to help and guide you. If neither of you have experience, you'll both be going through a learning curve and you will most likely end up in a mess, and life's too short for such mess. Find a supplier who is used to working with the same or similar content and/or contextual issues as your event has.

5. Appoint a supplier on the indicative value of their goods and/or how they feel to work with. Agree unit costs of goods if possible, or a framework and/or milestones and payment terms.

There is no reason whatsoever why you can't set hard budget limits at this stage if you're working to a fixed budget or want to limit expenditure. You will then be working with the supplier to design and develop the scope and specification of your event in line with this budget. I would always advise having this conversation before you make any final appointment, though, as each supplier will likely have a view on your budget. If you find yourself in a situation where you have one supplier telling you that your budget is more than adequate and another telling you it is nowhere near enough, assume the latter is right until you have hard evidence to the contrary or someone with relevant contextual experience has evaluated the budget and any quotes.

6. Management. Work with your supplier to develop a specification against the brief. Make sure you support them and confirm requirements once you've received their quotes, based on the terms, prices or framework you've agreed with them. This exercise gets you the expertise you need while making sure you're not getting ripped off as plans evolve and the event date approaches. I have successfully used or applied this approach myself for contracts ranging in price from a few thousand US dollars to approximately $40m. Of course, the larger the contract, the more checks and measures you need to put in place, but the process is identical regardless of contract size or complexity.

To give an example, my team and I once used this approach to source a supplier to help specify and then manufacture clothing and uniforms for an event. Early on in the planning, we had no idea how many staff, crew and performers would need clothes or uniforms, but we still needed the support of a contractor who could help guide our choices about materials, design, production times and suitability of different garments. We wanted a trusted, reputable partner, but we also wanted to make sure we weren't going to get ripped off once we came to agreeing costs and moving into production.

We issued a simple tender, asking for background information about each supplier's company and examples of relevant contextual experience that matched the event we were developing. We then asked for unit costs for typical garments. When we got the various tenders back, to be sure we were comparing like for like, we took examples from each of the tenders and asked each company responding to provide unit costs for them.

A few interviews later, checking the chemistry was right, agreeing milestones and pricing structures, we had our preferred partner, secure in the knowledge that we would get not just the right expertise, but also the right prices.

It is worth noting that almost every supplier who responded wanted to offer us VIK deals. We dealt with this separately (after pricing had been compared) as we wanted to be sure we were getting the best value before any VIK offers confused our judgment.

When you're procuring the goods you need for live events, the exercise doesn't end with the contracting stage. If what you're contracting is common, standard and has been provided many times before, there is less of a concern. However, if – and this is common – what you're contracting is bespoke, unusual or perhaps unprecedented, the suppliers need support, guidance and supervision from those with relevant contextual experience. Leaving a

contractor to their own devices may be a sound idea on paper, but it can be enormously risky in reality. You also need to make sure your suppliers have the relevant support if you're using suppliers who are not used to working under the time constraints live events create, or not used to the scale or quantities involved.

This point is well illustrated by the example of an event I was once leading. One element of this live event required a large amount of infrastructure to be installed in an extremely short space of time – nothing complicated in normal circumstances, but the scale and speed involved in delivering the live event made it complicated.

The contractor my team and I had awarded the task of delivering this requirement was world class and arguably the leader in their field. Over months of planning, we looked at every small detail of what we needed and everything that could go wrong. The contractor's plans were well considered and robust. However, as my team and I had relevant contextual experience, we knew that they had never done an event on this scale before. No one had.

We only had one chance to get it right. If the contractor failed, there wouldn't be the time to rectify it, regardless of whose fault it was. For this reason, at our own expense, and without the contractor knowing, my team and I had an entire team of reserve staff on standby to dive in and help if the contractor showed any sign of struggling. In addition, we ordered contingency equipment for the most mission-critical areas of activity.

Come the day of the event, the contractor did struggle, through no fault of their own. A combination of unforeseen circumstances simply made their task incredibly difficult, at which point, the reserve team was deployed to help and everything was delivered smoothly.

Contracting event requirements necessitates more than just a contract and agreement, especially when the task the contractors are being asked to do is unusual or unprecedented. This is why it's so important to have the core roles established from the outset, covered where necessary by people who have relevant contextual experience.

Procuring services

We've covered goods, but what if you're looking for services of some description?

Professional services are the myriad of disciplines and skills that hold an event together, from the people managing and coordinating it through to specialist expertise. These could be any professional service: designers, artists, event management experts, sponsorship experts, consultants, marketing experts, commercial support, accountants, lawyers, travel agents, administrators, choreographers, IT support, stage managers, dancers, singers, scriptwriters, interpreters... basically, people with a specific talent or expertise. They could also be software/systems that automate what people do: registration or data management, for example.

In this section, we're only talking about services. If you're actually looking for both expertise and the supply of goods in one package or contract, then you're looking for a turnkey solution. We will cover that topic in Chapter 8.

As we know, live events can be divided into two key components: content (the purpose of a live event) and context (everything necessary to deliver the content and bring it to life). Anyone we procure to provide services needs relevant content or contextual experience, and the two shouldn't be confused.

Nowhere can the use of terminology scupper things more than when you're buying or procuring people's or organisations' services. Unless you're looking for a provider of a specific and widely understood service, an accountant for example, it's best to avoid terminology (job titles) altogether if you can. Simply explain exactly what you want doing in layman's terms.

There are primarily five steps to finding the services you need.

1. Brief. Write a brief, detailing what you do and don't want (the latter point being just as important), how long you think you may need the service for, and any other information you can think of that paints as full a picture as possible regarding what you're looking for. Use plain English and outline the challenge, opportunity or role as you see it. Importantly, also explain who the service provider (be it an individual or company) will be reporting to and managing (if relevant). Ask for their fee or rates for their services. If you are looking to fill a full-time salaried role, you can either provide a guide salary and benefits or ask for salary expectations.

If you are looking to fill professional roles with volunteers, follow the same procedure. After all, volunteers will need to be accountable and deliver a professional service, too. You can clearly leave out the fees element, replacing it with benefits or incentives that would appeal to likely candidates.

Add any governance requirements and procedures to your brief that you deem necessary. These could be checks or questions about financial standing; their tax, visa or employment status; health and safety track record (if relevant); employee conditions (if you're hiring a company); sustainability management; quality assurance; your organisation's HR policies; or any other criteria important to you and/or appropriate to the size and type of the opportunity. Be realistic, though: too much governance or paperwork could put off your best candidate or company.

2. Distribute your brief or job description in whatever way works for you or your organisation, be that via headhunters (some headhunters service temporary positions), through your own network, across social media, traditional media, or anywhere appropriate for the type of role you're looking for.

3. Assess the responses you receive on the quality and value of the providers' services and any other criteria important to you: their ideas/ creativity, experience or solutions, for example. Look closely at any caveats, notes or exclusions. Conduct any necessary interviews or clarifications.

4. Check the service provider's or person's references if you're not familiar with them. If you're looking for someone for one of the key roles to head up a live event, then you need to make sure that they have relevant content or contextual experience. To recap:

• Project lead: contextual experience is most important

• Content lead: content experience is most important

• Physical/technical delivery: contextual experience is most important

• Logistics/operations: contextual experience is most important

If you are looking for service providers to fill any other roles, you will need to make a call on the experience they require. There is no black and white, but ideally, if you can find people with both content and contextual experience, that's fantastic. As a rule, though, I would always advocate looking for people with some contextual experience. This isn't always possible, of course, so if you need to bring in people who don't have contextual experience, they will need supporting by people who do where necessary, which will be an additional cost and consideration.

At the end of the day, you have to deliver. Remember everyone's watching and you've got that fixed deadline. It can be tempting to hire junior staff, interns or those with little experience but plenty of enthusiasm. This works well if, and only if, there are adequate resources to support or train them, and only if those resources have the time to support and train them.

The only time I would advocate involving people without relevant contextual experience is when you're looking for new ideas, creativity, specialist knowledge, inspiration, design, art or similar. In these cases, if you focus purely on content skills, it often results in far more impressive, innovative and creative ideas, unrestrained by contextual issues. The people you bring on board will still need relevant contextual support to turn their ideas into something tangible, though.

How can you tell if people really have the relevant content or contextual experience you require? There is no magic answer, but speaking to the right people who have worked with your applicants before is usually a good start. Ask the applicants questions that most people are afraid to ask, for example:

- What did you actually do?
- Did you do this or did you oversee people who did it for you?
- Did you do this or did you support (report in to) someone who took responsibility for it?
- How many people were involved in doing this?
- Who did you report to and who reported to you in this instance?

I call this the 'up and down test'. Unless the applicant has experience of doing what you need doing, they are not the right person for the role. If they had a team working for them doing what you need doing, they are not the right person. If they reported in to someone doing what you need doing, they are not the right person. If they did what you need doing but always had the support of far more people than they will have for your event, they may be the right person, but they will need to be closely monitored and possibly supported.

Ideally, you're looking for people who have done what you're looking for themselves. Roles and responsibilities can be vague when it comes to live events, and having been involved with a live event isn't itself proof or qualification of someone's experience.

You can then check all their claims with the references your applicants provide when you speak to them. When I am looking to fill leadership and management roles, I always try to find people who have worked for anyone senior I am interested in engaging. You can tell quite quickly how potential candidates work with and lead a team by the responses you get (or don't get) from people who have worked under them. If you get at least a general sense of professional respect, this is usually a good sign.

Make sure you're clear and unemotional about the difference between content and context. A great artist, designer or creative won't necessarily have the contextual experience to realise their creativity. Equally, someone who's produced a whole host of live events previously, with a wealth of contextual experience, won't necessarily have the skillset to create great content. It's always important to carry out the content and context checks.

The idea here is not to catch people out; it is to get the services you need. If you're looking for a particular service and you don't have the relevant experience yourself, it can be frustrating to find out once you've brought someone on board that you've ended up with the wrong skillset in place because you couldn't articulate what you wanted. The opposite is possible, too. Without relevant experience, you may think what you require is more complicated than it actually is and end up with a service provider who is overqualified and overpriced, and be overstaffed for what you need.

Finally, perform any governance checks you deem necessary.

5. Appointment. Agree terms or rates for your providers' services. Keep any arrangements flexible, unless you are certain about the quality of the providers' services and certain your plans won't change.

Things can and usually do change, so when you're buying services, flexibility is key. If you're looking for people to fill full-time roles, then keeping things flexible can be more difficult. This is one reason why most people I work with are kept on flexible contracts. It can be tempting to take people on full time or for long periods of time in return for favourable rates or fees, but this is dangerous unless you can be absolutely certain the service providers you're engaging are fabulous and your plans aren't going to change. It's not difficult to keep contracts flexible, as long as you provide some security for those you're engaging, so keep things simple. You'll get more sleep.

This guidance assumes you're looking for professional services: qualified or experienced personnel, be they paid, volunteers, or anything in between. If you want to consider using personnel without the content or contextual experience of having worked on a similar event before – junior staff, interns, or willing and available yet inexperienced personnel, for example – they are going to need either support, training or guidance. This is only going to come from people with the relevant experience who have the ability, desire and time to support, train or guide those without experience.

There is no doubt that many day-to-day non-specialist tasks on live events can be undertaken by almost anyone. There is also no doubt that people can learn skills quickly. There will be a learning curve, though, if you engage inexperienced people. And as we looked at in the 'Leadership' chapter, the pressures live events exert on the inexperienced can lead to mixed results. You need careful consideration, therefore, if you're going to use junior or inexperienced personnel. They may well be cheap (free, even) and plentiful, and learning and development is to be encouraged, but only if you or your team have the ability and the time, which will be significant, to develop and support such talent.

Summary

There are six types of procurement approaches for getting anything you need for your live event:

- Procuring goods with a specification
- Procuring goods without a specification
- Procuring services
- Procuring a flexible turnkey solution
- Procuring a fixed turnkey solution
- Procuring or finding a promoter

The live event procurement toolkit I have devised is the result of decades of experience of what does and doesn't work. However, the approaches to procuring goods and service that we have covered in this chapter, along with the approaches to procuring turnkey solutions that make up the content of the next chapter, are for your guidance only. They are not a set of hard and fast rules. You can use them literally, as I do, or as a framework, weaving in any specific requirements, human resources or procurement practices of your own.

Now we have covered the details of procuring goods and services, it's time to move on to something a bit more complex: the three approaches to procuring turnkey solutions.

8

A powerful toolkit to get you the live event you want, even if you don't know exactly what you want.

Chapter 8

Procurement Toolkit Part 2: Turnkey Solutions

Having provided in the previous chapter an overview of the six approaches in your procurement toolkit and detailing the first three – how goods and services are best procured – you have the background necessary to find turnkey solutions more effectively and efficiently.

This chapter focuses on the second three of these six approaches: how to procure turnkey solutions, and outsourcing complete events or separate parts of larger events in their entirety.

This starts by looking at what a turnkey solution is and how to avoid common issues that occur by assuming procuring turnkey events is like procuring turnkey packages in other sectors.

We then go on to look at how to find your perfect turnkey solution with confidence and clarity.

What are turnkey solutions?

A turnkey solution consists of a package of both services and goods. Your focus needs to be on finding the right service providers in the first instance.

Broadly speaking, there are three types of turnkey solutions. Firstly, there's the complete turnkey solution where you're looking for a live event to be designed and created from scratch, and then planned and delivered in its entirety. In other words, you are looking for an organisation to produce the event and deliver the production.

Secondly, there's the production only turnkey solution. You may know what you want and just need it planned and delivered. You are therefore the producer and you are looking for someone to deliver the production. Boundaries between these two can blur, of course, yet they are really quite different.

Finally, there's the type of turnkey solution for specific elements of an event. This is where you're simply looking for part of an event to be looked after.

Some examples of the complete turnkey solution:

• You own a brand that needs to launch a new project. You want strategy, consumer insights, ideas, and a magnificently designed event, so you're looking for an expert to create this. Once you're happy with their idea, you want them to plan and deliver your event in its entirety

• You want to put on some entertainment. The content needs creating, the show needs designing, and then it needs planning and delivering

Some examples of production only turnkey solutions:

• You are an artist and you know your content. You know what your stage show is going to look like, and you simply need a company to stage the event for you. You'll be producing it; you merely want it planned and delivered

- You represent a public body – a government department, for example – that wants to stage a state occasion, stunt or activation. If you know exactly what you want and you're looking after the content and design of the event, you're merely looking for an organisation to plan and deliver the production

- You represent a sports organisation that needs to stage a sporting event. You're developing, designing and leading it; you're merely looking for it to be planned and delivered by a production company or similar

Finally, some examples of turnkey solutions for specific elements of an event:

- You are producing, planning and delivering a concert, but want a company to produce, design and deliver an activation event to take place outside the stadium to entertain the queues as a turnkey solution

- You are producing and delivering a sporting event, but want to outsource the expo where sponsors will exhibit their wares as a turnkey solution

Know what you actually need from a turnkey solution before you start looking for one. It will make your life, and the lives of the people and organisations you approach, far easier. Ask yourself:

- Am I looking for ideas, content and delivery?

- Do I already have the ideas and content, and just need the production developed and delivered?

- Do I need specific parts of an event or activity designed or developed and then delivered?

Again, avoid industry-specific lingo. Simply use layman's terms and be clear with everyone on what you are looking for.

Common outsourcing mistakes

Before I go into detail on how best to procure (buy) a turnkey solution, let's look at how turnkey solutions are commonly outsourced. I have no hard data, but if my experience is typical, which I believe it is, this is the way 80–90% of live events around the world are outsourced, and it's just about the least effective way of outsourcing a live event.

This method involves putting out a brief, and then asking for a proposal and price in return. Sounds sensible, simple and straightforward, doesn't it? Let's look at an example of how such an approach works.

A woman – let's call her Claire – works for a large organisation which has just won a company of the year award. The CEO is so excited that he wants Claire to put on an event for the company's staff, clients and the media to celebrate. He wants a posh dinner, entertainment, fireworks; he wants to make a big speech; and as it'll be a work event, he wants networking meetings, too.

First, Claire must decide whether to produce the event internally or outsource it. Doing it internally, Claire can bring different people on board when she's ready, she'll have direct control over suppliers, and there won't be any price mark-ups or similar shenanigans.

However, Claire and her team are busy and producing events isn't really what they do, and a serious man in a position much higher than hers has told her that doing the event in house all sounds a bit risky. It'd be better to outsource it all, even if it will cost a little more than doing it internally, freeing up Claire's time and offsetting any risk.

Claire writes a brief detailing what the CEO wants and sends out a request for proposal (RFP), similar to a tender, inviting a few companies to compete for the work. After assessing the responses, Claire and her CEO decide they really like Shiny Communication Inc.'s proposal (this is an illustrative company name, and any similarity to a real company, past, present or future, is unintentional and purely coincidental). As a result, Claire gets the go-ahead to award this company the contract.

Everything starts well. A few weeks in, though, the CEO tells Claire that he wants to add a large experiential exhibition to showcase the company's widgets. This means amending Shiny Communication Inc.'s contract and cancelling the dinner to save money for the exhibition. The dinner was where Shiny Communication Inc. was going to make most of its profit, so its representative gets a bit grumpy and Claire has to talk them round. She really doesn't enjoy doing this and senses she's now not going to get the same level of care and support she may have received before from Shiny Communication Inc.

Next, it turns out Shiny Communication Inc. can't get permission for the event's fireworks display as it will be too noisy and the local residents have complained about the plans. Shiny Communication Inc.'s representative then admits to Claire that they thought this may happen. Claire, now furious, asks why they included it in the company's original proposal. Shiny Communication Inc.'s representative explains to Claire that as she had asked for it in the RFP, everyone pitching for the work had included it, and if Shiny Communication Inc. hadn't included it, its proposal wouldn't have looked as great as its competitors' proposals. It was a competition, after all.

Claire was distraught as she and the CEO had loved Shiny Communication Inc.'s proposal so much. Her CEO was furious and demanded they hire a world-famous superstar to sing at the event to add some impact, and that Shiny Communication Inc. should pay the superstar's fee, even though the superstar would cost more than the fireworks display would have cost. Claire and Shiny Communication Inc. end up having different points of view on who's to blame for what and who should pay for what.

With the event approaching rapidly, Claire and Shiny Communication Inc.'s representative are spending more time managing each other than focusing on the event. The serious man from upstairs has got involved again, too, given there are so many changes to the event and costs are spiralling out of control. Claire even tries to cancel the event, but the contract her organisation has with Shiny Communication Inc. means she has committed her organisation to spending a great deal of money already. Also, the whole company and the external media have been told about the event.

Claire now isn't getting much sleep. The final event bears little resemblance to the original idea that Claire and her CEO were so excited about, and once it is over, her only emotion is relief.

This fictitious example is based on real, and common, experiences. Most people who have either procured live events or provided them via a procurement process will recognise at least some of the issues in this example.

The problems all stem from trying to find the right group of people to design and produce an event and provide you with the expertise and guidance you need by asking companies to design and produce an event before they are appointed and able to undertake full due diligence. This sounds crazy, yet it is incredibly common.

You will also find many organisations who see nothing wrong with this approach to procurement, as it is what normally happens and seeing the issues it creates is just 'part of the game'.

You will also find many agencies and suppliers who are actually structured to both expect and, in turn, rightly, profit from this disorganised approach, knowing it will happen and knowing how to capitalise on it. There's a saying: 'There's good money to be made from chaos.'

Neither of these points make it right, though, especially when distracting precious resource and talent from focusing on creating the maximum impact possible and reducing the value of what you're buying because of inherent inefficiencies is so unnecessary. It's all completely avoidable.

This approach to outsourcing turnkey solutions, as far as I can tell (and I've been living and studying this for nearly two decades now), offers you just two benefits if you're the client. But are they really benefits? Let's have a look.

1. In theory, you've got a price for something. You have what you think is a price for what you think you're getting, and it sits nicely in your budget. Therefore, you can move on to the next thing.

However, unless an event is formulaic, until it is designed and planned in detail, you simply can't know the price, which means that you may face more costs or need to change plans, or that the turnkey solution you've purchased may be compromised as your supplier or agency rebalance the fixed turnkey budget to mitigate escalating costs or scope variations. Or you may find you're paying over the odds if those working for you (and all those who competed for the work) have built in hefty hidden contingencies knowing full well they'll have levels of uncertainty to deal with.

2. You've offset the risks. You believe the risks associated with the event are covered by a third party, protecting you and your organisation. However, while a contract may protect you legally after an event, it won't help get your event delivered in the manner you expect if cracks appear in the planning close to your immovable event deadline.

An organisation may know it needs expertise to help it conceive, develop and design an event before it even looks at how the event may be delivered. Yet due to the way the organisation's procurement guidelines are structured, or simply because the organisation doesn't know there's a viable alternative, it seeks a complete turnkey solution, knowing full well that the event will change, possibly beyond all recognition, between the point the contract is awarded and the point at which it's delivered.

To give you a real example of this, a large organisation put out a tender for an event management company to design and create a high-profile live public event. Those tendering had to respond with fully worked-up visuals and plans of their proposals, specifications and costs. This effectively meant planning much of the event prior to being appointed, at their own commercial risk. A number of agencies responded with their visions and proposals, accompanied by *estimated* costs, and the organisation appointed a winner, chosen primarily on cost.

As planning began, it transpired that the organisation (the client) liked the ideas in the proposal that won the contract, but by and large, it wanted its own ideas delivered. What followed was months of wrangling, given the fact that the client organisation had awarded the contract based on the original turnkey proposal.

When I asked why the client organisation had taken this approach to finding a company to work with, the answer was that its procurement guidelines only allowed it to move forward once it had a cost for a complete solution. If there wasn't a scope and a total price next to it on a proposal, there would be no acceptable way for the organisation to purchase it.

Consider what you're asking for in a turnkey solution. You're asking, effectively, for some type of overview, picture, design, proposal or plan for a live event based on a brief you've set out, and a price next to it to develop it and deliver it. In other words, you're asking someone to develop and plan something and then deliver it, and you'd like to know what it's going to cost.

Think about this logically, though. How can anyone know what a live event is going to cost until it's planned and developed? Many will argue that an experienced organisation should know what things cost. This is true, but it's not the cost of 'things' that may vary; it's the specifications, scope, external forces, politics, creative decisions, venue- or site-specific issues that may change, and with it the type or number of 'things' needed can change. In turn, all these factors may change the costs, so you're effectively asking for a fixed price for a variable specification.

This results in one of three things happening:

1. The supplier or agency will spend a considerable amount of time managing you to make sure, as the specification evolves, that it remains deliverable to the quote.

This is time that you'll be paying for, either directly or through compromise in other areas as the supplier or agency adjusts plans to maintain a profit margin.

2. You will needlessly spend a considerable amount of your own time managing the supplier or agency to make sure they still deliver what you expect, as your expectations evolve, to the quote they originally gave.

3. You and your agency or supplier will agree contract changes, variations, or the use of contingency funds outside any budget (or quote) given. But if this is the case, what was the point of asking for a price or quote in the first place? The answer usually is to compare value with other people who were bidding for the tender, or to try to understand what a live event would cost. This is just about the most inefficient way possible of assessing value as you're not comparing anything comparable.

If the live event you're asking for a quote on is formulaic, with no likelihood of change, then the approach of putting out a tender or RFP works just fine. These are typically live events such as straightforward conferences or seminars in well-equipped conference centres or venues, concerts in known locations with known costs, or similar. Even with these straightforward events, though, things can often change, so read on.

You can't buy turnkey live event solutions the same way you buy or procure anything else. That doesn't mean it has to be complicated, risky or hard work, though. There is a simple way; an efficient and enjoyable way.

Let's look at how you can best get hold of turnkey solutions with minimal fuss.

Procuring a flexible turnkey solution

The flexible turnkey solution is best used when it's likely your event will evolve between brief and delivery. In other words, this is the solution you will need most of the time.

To give you a few examples:

- Maybe your event is in a public space, and the considerations of businesses, residents, emergency services and public (municipal) authorities have to be taken into consideration during the planning stages
- Maybe you have a number of key stakeholders who need to be involved throughout the early stages and well into planning
- Maybe you don't know what you need yet, so you want people to come up with ideas, insights, strategies or designs, and then go on to deliver the live event
- Maybe you just want some design ideas to find the right creative agency and work with them to develop and deliver the live event
- Maybe you are looking for an organisation to retain for a period of time to help you create, produce and deliver a number of live events

All of these examples illustrate that it's almost impossible to create a brief that can be developed and quoted for accurately. Plans or ideas usually change considerably as the process evolves. In fact, in twenty years I can't think of a single occasion where plans haven't evolved between the initial idea and the event being delivered. And I can think of only a handful of occasions when everyone involved in the event has had complete control over all decisions, ideas and requirements, and hence the costs.

The goal with a flexible turnkey solution is to find the right organisation (or group of organisations) to help you. You need to focus primarily on the services the organisations can provide: the expertise that their people bring you. It will usually always be possible to find cheaper or better value goods, so it's the expertise you need to check and secure in the first place.

It is all too common when you're searching for a turnkey live event solution to give the contract to the organisation that can provide the cheapest goods. If you're looking for specialist expertise, be that creative, technical, operational or strategic, this can be a false economy. It would be akin to selecting an architect based on how cheaply they could provide concrete.

Let's look at the flexible turnkey approach step by step.

1. Brief. Write a brief, detailing what you do and don't want. Provide as much information as you can, using plain English and avoiding industry-specific jargon or acronyms wherever possible. Include location or location ideas, dates or date options, timings or possible timings, and details of the audience and participants. Terms like 'creative', 'innovative', 'high quality',

'wow' and 'best in the world' alone are extremely subjective and won't help an organisation develop ideas and designs for you. Provide details or examples of what you consider creative, innovative, high quality and best in the world to mean. The more information you can provide, the better.

Ask for an organisation's fee or rates for its services. Ask how it will guarantee to procure the best value goods. For most goods, the best way the organisation can demonstrate this is by providing you with competitive quotes before they (and in turn, you) place any orders. If this becomes unwieldy because of a large number of contracts, you could just ask for approval on quotes for contracts over a certain value.

It will be difficult for organisations to provide competitive quotes for specialist goods, such as those that require research and development. In these instances, you want to understand how the organisation you're appointing will source these goods and monitor and manage the contractors undertaking this specialist work. This book provides guidance on what they should be doing.

Provide a guideline budget for everything (goods and services), even if you provide a number below what you actually have to spend, otherwise you will be wasting your own and other people's time and money. I realise that providing a guideline budget goes against the grain of many people's comfort zones and organisations' approaches. If this really isn't possible, provide examples of similar events or activities that you know the cost of to give some level of realistic expectation with regard to scale and quality.

If you're considering conducting a procurement exercise to determine feasibility or budget, don't. There is an inherent conflict of interests in trying to determine the feasibility or budget of an event or elements of an event using a turnkey procurement solution. Any organisation competing

for a tender is unlikely to tell you everything you need to hear about the cost of your event. And almost every organisation knows that the cost (or more accurately, the scope) of an event goes up once the tender has been awarded. Unless what you aim to do has never been done before, which is rare, it will cost you far less in the long run and be far safer simply to pay what will be a nominal amount of money for specialist knowledge rather than use a tendering process to determine an event's feasibility or cost. In most cases this will likely cost you far less to do than you think.

Return on investment (ROI) is a topic that could fill an entire book. You will find many self-proclaimed experts on the art of event ROI, but simply asking an organisation to demonstrate how they'll measure ROI won't get you very far.

If ROI is relevant or important to you, you need to define what it is you're looking to achieve with an event. The organisation can then articulate how they'll measure those factors, rather than the 'event' as a whole. Are you looking for sales leads, audience comprehension, satisfaction, consumer engagement/interactions, publicity, customer or behaviour insights...or anything else? If you're looking for ROI measured in any form, you need to specify what it is you want measured. Why are you holding the event in the first place? Organisations will then be able to offer better ROI guidance, if this factor is relevant or important to you.

Add any governance criteria and procedures to your brief that you deem necessary. These could be checks or questions about financial standing, health and safety, employee conditions, sustainability management, quality assurance, or any other criteria important to you and/or appropriate to the size and type of the opportunity.

2. Distribute your brief in whatever way works for you or your organisation. You may circulate it online to organisations you've selected or have had recommended. You may run a formal public tendering process. You may ask friends and/or colleagues to distribute it. It may even all be done verbally, if that works for you, for a smaller event or requirement.

3. Assess the responses you receive on the quality and value of services and any other criteria important to you, for example ideas/creativity, experience, credibility, solutions etc. Look closely at any caveats, notes or exclusions. Assess each organisation's process for providing the best value goods once you've developed the specification together. Conduct any interviews or clarifications necessary.

4. Check references the organisations responding provide if you're not familiar with them. Conduct the up and down check. Did the applicants actually do what they say they have done previously, or just a part of it? Did they either report up to people who did what you need, or have people beneath them who did what you need doing?

Check to make sure the team each organisation has in place covers each of the key roles. Can you identify:

- Which **one** person will be responsible for leading the event (contextual experience is key)?
- Which **one** person will be responsible for its content (content experience is key)?
- Which **one** person will be responsible for its technical delivery (contextual experience is key)?
- Which **one** person will be responsible for the logistics and operations (contextual experience is key)?

If the event is a number of smaller or separate events, check the key roles are in place for each part. Conduct the content and context checks. If you are looking for help with the content of your event, the solution will need relevant content experience. If you or your team are leading on this, it is less important. If you are looking for help with delivering or facilitating your event, the solution will need relevant contextual experience of similar events.

Perform any governance checks you deem necessary.

5. Appointment. Agree terms, fees or rates for the turnkey solution's services. Agree cash flow payment terms. Then, separately, agree how goods will be secured at the best value and on what terms, and that they shouldn't be contracted without your approval if you want to maintain control. You may want to set this up for contracts over a certain value, to save you from getting swamped in every small expense. Ask to see copies (or for the right to see copies) of all invoices or those over a certain value, and for details of how the budget will be reconciled with any unused funds returned.

If you prefer, you can contract all third parties directly, with the agency or organisation overseeing this process, procuring and managing the contracts on your behalf. This gives you the security you may want, it removes any commercial or credit risk the agency may face, and it can work well provided the organisation is empowered with the control they will need over the third parties.

Agree an overall project/target budget. You can even incentivise (reward) those you appoint for trying to save money or reduce the budget by splitting the proceeds of any genuine reductions. This gives you a flexible arrangement while ensuring you're getting the best value and capping any budgets. Most importantly, though, it means you will have a team working with you, transparently and openly.

6. Management. Only make variations to the services you and your turnkey solution provider have agreed if the original scope changes, and only release money for goods once the provider has followed the agreed process for providing them. The result of this process is that you will have a group of people you can work and develop ideas and plans with. You'll know you're not going to get ripped off by them for any of the goods as everyone will be working towards a target budget.

An example of when I used the flexible turnkey solution incredibly successfully was in procuring event and creative agencies to provide entertainment and activations for a corporate festival. My team and I knew we needed all manner of entertainment and activations, but we wanted to find the most appropriate ideas without limiting creativity too much. We also knew we didn't want to get ripped off. It would be no good to anyone if we spent months developing ideas with an organisation only to find we couldn't then afford our plans. Yet we also knew plans would change. Often.

I issued a tender and sent it out to numerous relevant organisations, making it crystal clear what the event was and who the audience was, and detailing the contextual items: location, restrictions, scale and similar.

I also made it clear I was looking for ideas that would likely change as plans evolved. I asked those willing to respond to detail the entertainment and activations they felt answered the brief, stipulating a guide budget. Had I not provided a budget, those responding would have been missing a key piece of contextual information that would render the process largely useless, as we wouldn't know what we could afford, or what our money would buy. However, given how early on in its development this event was, and given the many variables still in play, I provided a guide budget significantly less than what I knew we had available. This gave me room to manoeuvre should other contextual factors change.

Once the team and I had selected the companies we wanted to partner with based on their ideas and quotes (estimates), we worked with them to provide exactly what they had offered, or modify it as and when areas of activity could be enhanced or needed changing. Importantly, my team

and I had the contextual experience to know with reasonable certainty whether our additional funds could be released.

This approach provided me with a method to find the right companies to work with: a method that kept me firmly in control financially, free of the risks of any cost overruns, and allowed me to scale the value and impact of the event up and down as it evolved.

If you work for a large or heavily regulated organisation, it's possible your internal procurement guidelines will state that you need to know the whole cost of an event before you can award a contract. If you are burdened with this governance, the procurement processes are actually doing the opposite of what they've been designed to do: secure what you need at the best value. I have procured numerous live events and event requirements for organisations with such governance, and have usually found a way to make this approach work. Provided you make your case well, mitigating concerns and risks with science and proven approaches, you can often get everyone in your organisation's procurement and legal teams on board with what you're trying to achieve. Just make sure that the process is led by people with relevant contextual expertise.

If you really can't change your organisation's internal procurement practices or find creative ways of finding the solutions you need, though, you'll have to use the fixed turnkey solution, which we will look at next.

Procuring a fixed turnkey solution

A fixed turnkey solution is best used when you know your event's requirements will not change, either by decisions you make or external forces or circumstances, between the brief and delivery – which is rare.

If you're looking for a turnkey solution for a live event that is formulaic or that's happened many times before, the fixed approach is perfect. Examples are a straightforward conference or seminar in a hotel ballroom, a small or modular exhibition stand at a tradeshow, or a concert in a venue that has hosted the same type of concert time and time again.

The best way to secure a fixed turnkey solution is as follows.

1. Brief. Detail what you do and don't want. When turnkey solution providers apply to work with you, ask for the price of both their services and any goods you require. Provide as much information as you can, use plain English, and avoid industry-specific jargon or acronyms wherever possible. The more information you can provide, the better.

Provide a guideline budget, even if you provide a number below what you actually have.

If you're considering conducting a procurement exercise to determine feasibility or budget, don't. An organisation competing for your work will more often than not focus on good news and cheaper prices rather than home truths. Even if you give those competing for the tender the opportunity to ask questions or present alternative ideas, their incentive will be to win the work, so there will be an inherent limit to how honest their advice and feedback will be.

Add any criteria for the event that you may want measuring or assessing if ROI is important to you or if you want specific actions or statistics recorded in some way.

Add any governance criteria and procedures to your brief that you deem necessary.

2. Distribute your brief in whatever way works for you or your organisation. You may circulate it online, run a formal public tendering process, or ask friends and/or colleagues to distribute it.

3. Assess the responses you receive on the quality and value of services and any other criteria important to you, for example ideas/creativity, experience, credibility, solutions etc. Look closely at any caveats, notes or exclusions. Conduct any interviews or ask for any clarifications necessary.

4. Check the references the organisations responding provide if you're not familiar with them. Conduct the up and down check, that is: did the applicants actually do what they say they have done previously, or just a part of it? Or did they either report up to people who did what you need doing, or did they have people beneath them who did what you need doing?

Check to make sure the team each organisation has in place covers each of the key roles. Can you identify:

- Which **one** person will be responsible for leading the event (contextual experience is key)?
- Which **one** person will be responsible for its content (content experience is key)?
- Which **one** person will be responsible for its technical delivery (contextual experience is key)?
- Which **one** person will be responsible for the logistics and operations (contextual experience is key)?

If the event is a number of smaller or separate events, check the key roles are in place for each part. Conduct the content and context checks. If you are looking for help with the content of your event, whoever you contract will need relevant content experience.

If you or your team are leading on this, this is less important. If you are looking for help with delivering or facilitating your event, whoever you contract will need relevant contextual experience of similar events.

Perform any governance checks you deem necessary.

5. Appointment. Agree terms, fees, rates or prices for everything. Agree the process for any scope or budget variations both during pre-production, when there will be plenty of time available, and nearer and during the event, when changes may need to be made and agreed almost instantaneously. Agree cash flow and/or payment terms.

6. Management. Make sure any variations to the contract, if they happen, are agreed by you before they are implemented. If it's likely there will be many variations, it will be easier and cheaper to use the flexible turnkey solution.

Procuring a promoter

If you have rights – commercial rights, marketing rights or any other rights – that a third party could exploit (sell for money), you can award those rights to a 'promoter', who will take on the responsibility and risk of delivering your event, in line with any agreed terms or guidelines, in return for the opportunity to make a profit.

They may do this at no cost to you, a reduced cost to you, on a profit/revenue-share basis, or in any combination of the three – subject to the type of event and value of the rights you're offering.

A promoter may well be an event agency or someone who has an event team. Terminology, again, is irrelevant as not all such companies will be called promoters; I use the word only for reference.

You need to be realistic about the value of the rights you offer any promoter, and make sure whoever you appoint is capable of both providing or finding the money and delivering an event.

This route of outsourcing an event to a promoter rather than doing it yourself or with your own team at your own risk is only worth considering if an event has a track record of commercial success, or if you can either demonstrate, ideally independently, that the event has commercial viability, or enough people with relevant contextual experience believe it has merit.

If you're looking to find a promoter, follow these steps:

1. Brief. Write a brief, detailing the marketing rights, commercial rights or any other rights you have to offer and what you'd like in return. A brief could be a simple outline of the event, including guidance on what the event will be and how it should be staged, along with example sponsorship packages and ticketing prices for a seminar or small conference. At the other end of the spectrum, for a major sporting event, for example, where you want different cities competing for the rights to host (promote and deliver) your event, the brief would encompass detailed creative and technical requirements along with commercial expectations and opportunities.

This will be part brief and part sales pitch, as you will need to outline the commercial potential of the event with as much evidence as possible.

Add any governance criteria and procedures to your brief that you deem necessary.

2. Distribute your brief in whatever way works for you or your organisation.

3. Assess the responses you receive on the quality and value of services and any other criteria important to you. Look closely at any caveats, notes or exclusions. Conduct any interviews or clarifications necessary.

4. Check references the promoters who are responding provide if you're not familiar with them. Most importantly, check if they can sell. If you are relying on the successful promoter to find sponsorship, funding, customers or investment in return for your rights, they need to have proven selling and marketing ability. This needs considerable attention. Ask if each organisation can sell. Is selling what its team does normally? If the promoter intends to partner with another organisation that will do the selling, you need to know this. You need to know which organisation they intend to partner with and establish the credentials of that organisation separately. Whether it's finding participants, attracting an audience, securing funding, landing sponsors, or finding money through any other means, make sure the promoter, and any individual or organisation they partner with, has a track record in this area.

Once you know your promoter can sell, you then need to know if they can produce and deliver the event. Don't confuse selling and producing. The two skills, or services, are worlds apart.

If a promoter intends to outsource the producing and delivery side of the live event, ensure you and they go through the guidance I have outlined to procure or appoint the organisation they choose. Conduct the up and down checks and the content and context test.

Perform any governance checks you deem necessary.

5. Appointment. Agree terms. If your event is critical, ie, it has to happen, include break clauses that allow you to find another solution should the promoter fail to obtain sponsorship, marketing, funding, attendees or participants in good time.

6. Management. Review the promoter's progress regularly wherever it's appropriate or possible. If you have concerns, apply the governance, selling, and content and context checks again with more rigour and make any changes necessary.

Summary

A turnkey solution consists of a package of both services and goods. Your focus needs to be on finding the right service providers in the first instance. However, the way many people and organisations outsource their live events to turnkey service providers is often fundamentally flawed. Asking for a proposal and cost for something that has not yet been developed or planned, in order to find the people to develop and plan it requires people to develop and plan it before they've been appointed to develop and plan it – a paradox that – as we've seen – leads to a great many unnecessary problems for both sides.

Additionally, if you are looking for valuable information, detailed or considered strategies, or design or concepts, there is merit in shortlisting two or three companies before asking them to embark on the work you require for your live event. The quality of responses you will get will be greatly improved as the risk to reward ratio will be more favourable to them. In other words, the companies you approach will know they are not competing against dozens of other companies.

If you are looking for creative work or design solutions and ideas, while it's not common in the live event world, you could offer a modest competition design fee. This will likely see a great improvement in the quality of the responses you receive.

Whether you're procuring turnkey services or just the goods or services you need, make sure that the demands of your procurement approach are realistic. Too much regulatory or compliance documentation at the tender stage will put some organisations off. Depending on the nature of your requirement, you may therefore be losing great value and ideas from companies, perhaps smaller companies, that are more than capable of servicing your requirements, but are deterred by your demands. You can always do further due diligence once you decide you're interested in a company's proposal.

Whichever approach you adopt, don't lose sight of the end goal. Live events are inherently exciting. You want any people, teams or suppliers you bring on board to be as engaged and excited as you are, if not more so. Anything you can do to ease processes or support people will make them far more likely to go the extra mile when the work to produce and deliver a live event becomes intense. It is, after all, people rather than processes that are the most important components of any live event.

A quick reference guide summarising all six approaches to procuring everything you need for a live event can be found at www.TheFactsOfLive.com.

Now you know how to procure the goods, services and/or turnkey solutions you will need, how and when do you use these procurement approaches in an event's continually changing lifecycle?

9

How live events are conceived, procured and produced to create the greatest value and impact.

Chapter 9

Your Live Event

In this final chapter we first address two common conundrums. Just how do you go about finding or creating new ideas, harnessing creativity or driving innovation? And if you're looking to create a live event or need one to service an objective you've identified, how do you judge whether to do it in house or outsource it?

The ridiculously simple live event lifecycle, or 'live cycle,' pulls all the information and guidance in *The Facts Of Live* together, providing yet further clarity on where, when and how to use the foundations and principles we've looked at.

To round things off, the book concludes with a summary of all the ways *The Facts Of Live* can support you or those you bring on board to conceive, procure and produce live events to deliver the biggest impact.

Ideas, creativity and innovation

No one wakes up in the morning and says, 'Do you know what? I really want a live event.' What you actually want is to sell something, communicate something or entertain people.

Unless your event is simply to facilitate existing content – a straightforward sporting event, for example – developing a live event to move people to buy stuff, think differently, understand a message or be amazed by fantastic entertainment usually means you need one or all of the following:

- A strategy
- Insights into customer behaviour
- Innovative or interesting ideas
- Unique, intriguing or inspiring creativity or designs

It can be tempting to focus solely on people from the event world, as it were, when you're looking for these things. This can work, and often does. It isn't your only route, though. If you are an event agency looking for ideas for a client or you represent an organisation looking for insights, creativity, innovation or anything similar, you have the entire world at your disposal.

A reason the core team of four roles works so well is that it marries those with contextual experience and those who have content experience. The content – ideas, strategy, creativity, innovation or anything similar – can come from anywhere, though new ideas and innovation rarely come from doing the same as you did before. Someone with relevant and proven contextual experience, whether they're the project lead or a separate creative director with contextual experience, can work with ideas from anywhere to turn them into tangible live-event propositions. They can also work with an idea that has merit but is not tangible to develop something that is.

I have worked with artists with no event experience at all who have come up with incredible designs for events. I have found innovative technical solutions and ideas for live events in sectors that have nothing to do with events whatsoever. As big data evolves as an industry, it provides enormous insights and creativity that you can develop or evolve, too.

The world is vast and varied. If you or those you bring on board are looking for ideas and innovations, either for your own live events or for your clients', it can pay huge dividends to do what most people aren't doing: look to other fields and types of expertise for inspiration.

All you need is an initial spark of an idea that a team of experienced event professionals can work with. The right contextual experts in the team will be adept at merging the myriad of different creative disciplines required to produce a live event, which may sometimes compete or conflict.

If you have the opposite problem and are trying to do too many things or have too many ideas, be brutal and strip them back. It is far better to do one thing well than half-heartedly attempt too many different things, with your product, message or art getting watered down in the process.

The team structure of four key roles adopting the principles I have outlined throughout *The Facts Of Live* will mean you will have the right people in play and able to focus fully on creative direction and/or solutions to ensure ideas are given the attention they need to shine, with far less risk of becoming watered down. You want, after all, to create the maximum impact with your live event: the most powerful medium you have to do so.

In or out?

Ideas and creativity aside, one of the first decisions anyone has to make when they need a live event is whether to do it in house, outsource it, or adopt a hybrid approach, merging the two. If you are undecided, the advice in *The Facts Of Live* should provide more than enough insights for you to make a judgment call on this.

If you have a pre-existing team or you appoint people to produce your event in house (either full time or temporarily), provided they have the right content and contextual experience, this is often going to be the most cost-effective solution. However, if you and/or your organisation aren't set up with the processes and practices to support the fluid nature of a live event fully, this approach may be counterproductive. An external organisation may be more nimble and reactive.

A common reason individuals and organisations give for outsourcing their live events is the belief that an external organisation which produces many events a year will have better buying power with suppliers and subcontractors. This may have been the case at some point in history, but with the transparency and competitive landscape of the modern age we live in, I have seen little evidence of this being the case nowadays, if the entire cost of procuring and acquiring goods and services is taken into account. An external organisation may be adept at negotiating deals, but if you have the right content and contextual expertise in house, you'll have people who can negotiate just as well.

While there is certainly no hard and fast rule, I would tend to advise you to consider producing your live events in house (with either permanent or temporary expertise) when:

- You are on a tight budget
- You have an event you want to develop, nurture and improve iteratively yourself, such as a festival, trade show or sporting event

- You have a number of repeat or identical events you produce year in, year out
- You have an event that you consider extremely confidential or sensitive
- You want a live event that is primarily artistic or creative, for example a concert, performance art, theatre or other entertainment, where you want to nurture talent and trust, and develop ideas and solutions together, building chemistry between all members of the team over time

Even if you are producing an event in house, you or your team could adopt a hybrid approach, keeping the leadership, design, management and planning in house, but outsourcing the delivery or production of specific requirements to your team's specification and under your team's direction.

Producing events in house, you will almost certainly be outsourcing the goods you need, unless you purchase everything. Servicing, maintenance, storage and transportation can often make purchasing goods considerably more expensive than hiring them. You will almost certainly have to purchase bespoke items, though, such as specific software, specialist technology, or custom-fabricated scenery and staging.

Again, there are no hard and fast rules, but I would tend to advise you to outsource an entire live event when:

- You or your organisation have no capacity or interest in doing it in house
- You want specialist knowledge, insight, strategic support, or creativity that you've identified in an external organisation
- You want fresh or different ideas and thinking

There is a third option, which is to set up a new company or subsidiary company, the sole aim of which is to produce and deliver a live event or events. However, I would only ever advise setting up a subsidiary company for a one-off event if the event is extremely complex, large, or requires independence. Major sporting events and vast, long-running cultural festivals tend to be the most common examples. Also, if you intend to start an annual festival, regular sporting event or a regular conference series, you'll be creating what amounts to a separate business, which could benefit from being a new or subsidiary company.

This is certainly not the most cost-effective solution for one-off events. It is, however, a solution favoured by stakeholders and funding partners when they have a considerable amount of money and reputation at stake. You can create a separate or new company with specific processes to reassure the stakeholders that the governance and transparency they require are in place.

Whichever route you choose, though, be sure you use the relevant content and contextual expertise to consider the options.

The live cycle

The Facts Of Live lifecycle, or live cycle, shown in Figure 9.1, illustrates how everything we have discussed in this book comes together.

Idea. Either you, someone in your organisation or a client have come up with an idea for a live event or one that needs a live event. You want to sell something, communicate something, or entertain, or perhaps all three.

Tipping Point. When you have made the decision to move forward with the idea, or at least to attempt the idea, you're at the tipping point. It's at this point you need to put the right team and expertise with relevant content and contextual experience in place.

Consult the tipping point choices to double check and determine the best approach for you to adopt. Refer to the tipping point choices chart in Chapter 7.

Services. The first thing you need is services. You need your core team of four key roles in place, and then any further resources you require. If you don't have these resources already, you'll need to find them. Follow the procurement approach we detailed in Chapter 7 to find services if you're looking to produce your event within your organisation, or consult Chapter 8 for a turnkey solution if you've chosen to outsource your event. If you have chosen the turnkey solution route, focus on services first. You need the talent with relevant content and contextual experience before anything else. Refer to the team and event structure explanations in Chapters 2 and 3 for more details.

Goods. As plans for the event progress, you are going to need goods: all the equipment, infrastructure and physical requirements, venues, content production, and any other elements. If you or your team are producing the event, then you will use one of the approaches we've looked at to procure goods. If you've chosen a turnkey solution, the goods you need will be procured by your solution provider.

See the procurement approaches in Chapters 7 and 8 for reference.

Review. Nearly all live events evolve and change as design, development and planning progress. Sometimes the changes are minor: a slight alteration in equipment specification, for example. On other occasions, events can expand with additional activities, ancillary and sub-events, or transform beyond all recognition.

Review your event's progress regularly. If there are significant changes or new requirements, move back up the cycle to Step One and assess these changes or requirements as you would if you were starting from scratch.

Repeat this review and cycle as often as necessary.

Live event. Once you've completed all the work above, you and your team will be in delivery mode. It's time to deliver your live event.

If you have followed the approaches, principles and methods detailed in *The Facts Of Live*, your live event will have maximum impact for the best value possible and with all risks either mitigated or minimised.

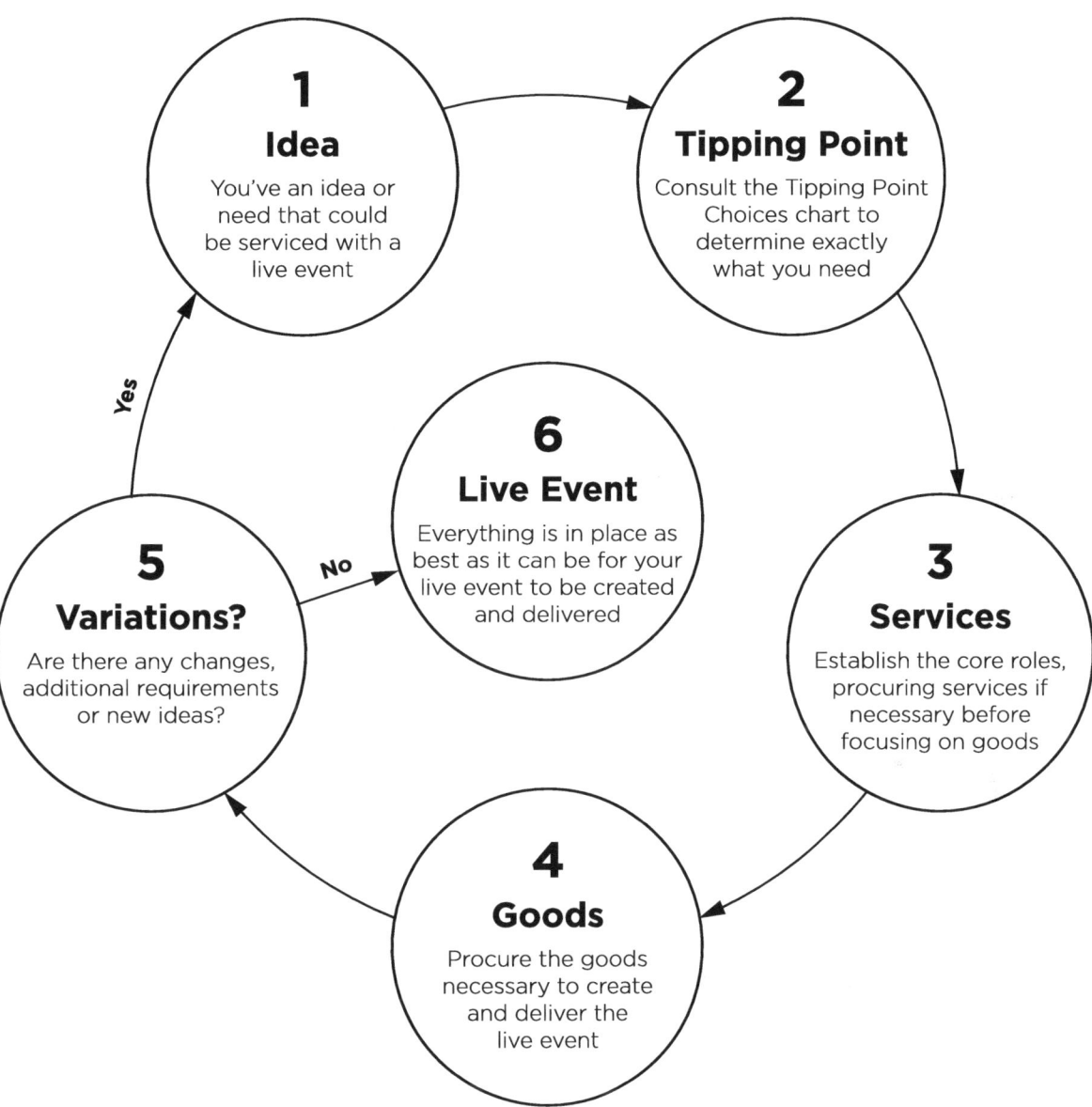

1
Idea
You've an idea or need that could be serviced with a live event

2
Tipping Point
Consult the Tipping Point Choices chart to determine exactly what you need

3
Services
Establish the core roles, procuring services if necessary before focusing on goods

4
Goods
Procure the goods necessary to create and deliver the live event

5
Variations?
Are there any changes, additional requirements or new ideas?

6
Live Event
Everything is in place as best as it can be for your live event to be created and delivered

Yes

No

Figure 9.1: Live event lifecycle – live cycle

Summary

The Facts Of Live has detailed how live events are most effectively conceived to create the best value and impact. By recognising the impact of decisions made at the tipping point, you can dramatically affect the path your live event takes as it evolves. Getting the right people in the right place at the right time will always set a live event on firm foundations.

The Facts Of Live then illustrated how live events are procured, given the uniquely fluid and changeable environment in which they develop. This guidance focused squarely on achieving the best value possible by making sure everyone's time, effort, money and talent go into the craft and needs of producing an incredible live event. We looked at what goes into producing a live event, the environment in which it is designed, developed and delivered, and how to get the best out of everyone involved. It is people who produce live events, and when they're empathetically led, empowered and supported, these people will have far greater value and impact.

There are common issues that you need to address in order for your live events to return the most value and create the biggest impact possible. Poor creativity, ideas getting watered down, lack of innovation, or wondering where or how to find the best creative talent or ideas can all negatively impact your event.

Ideas can come from anywhere. Just because you're producing a live event, it doesn't mean all your ideas are going to come from, or need to come from, the live event ideas people. If you're looking for genuinely new ideas or innovations, find people whose thinking you like – people with relevant content experience – and couple them with those who have relevant contextual experience to harness those ideas and turn them into something tangible for a live event. If you're outsourcing everything, ask those you're handing the task over to for their ideas or how they'll approach the task. New ideas and different thinking tend to come from approaching different people.

Make sure you find and engage with people who have the new ideas and different thinking your event needs.

Once you have your ideas, though, there is a risk that they may become watered down with the inevitable financial, practical and operational realities of a live event. This is where it's so important to have the core team of four roles involved from the outset. This marriage of roles, each filled by someone with the correct content and/or contextual experience, will ensure a project is feasible from the outset. Your event lead, creative lead, production (technical) lead and operations lead will then work together, aligned to maintain the creative integrity or direction of a live event throughout the entire process.

Most live events are going to change and evolve over time before they are delivered, and just hoping they won't is a recipe for disaster. The unique set of circumstances live events exist in makes the process of conceiving, producing and delivering them a

flexible and moveable beast. This is why relevant content and contextual experience is the single most important aspect to have in place as early as feasibly possible. You need the right people in the right place at the right time: experts who will know how best to lead the many moving parts.

Traditional project management and procurement approaches are difficult to apply to live events effectively. You can, though, combine them with the simple-to-use and clear toolkit in *The Facts Of Live* to find, secure or procure anything you could possibly need, whether you know what you need or just have an idea. If your organisation has existing practices or governance that you need to adhere to, you can use the toolkit as a starting point, then weave the existing governance requirements into the relevant process.

You need the right people in place to help work out what further resources a live event needs (if any). If you don't have the relevant contextual experience to know this already, find the people who do. Live events need leadership. A group of enthusiastic people around a table, in a committee or in a team, is not what will guide the numerous stakeholders, conflicting agendas and evolving expectations of a live event most effectively. Whether it's the person leading a whole live event or just part of it, you need strong, authoritative and empowered leadership in all the key roles. It is essential. An unguided live event lacking in strong leadership will drift from one place to another, lurching between one issue and the next.

In all but the rarest of incidents, most risks can be identified long before a live event sees the light of day. People with the relevant content and contextual expertise will be able to identify which risks are most likely or will have the biggest impact and how best to mitigate them. Prioritise these risks before considering the less likely or impactful risks that could arise.

The single biggest step you can take to minimise all risks is to make the right choices at the tipping point. As with any other professional venture, getting the right experts or advice early on is a wise move. Live events should be no different. Once you've managed or mitigated risks and developed a clear path forward, you and those you bring on board will be far more in control of your live event.

The first task in creating a live event with the most value is to identify the point or purpose of the event. If you can't work out why you're staging a live event, it's unlikely to provide any value. There may well be far more effective ways to deliver the objectives you're aiming to achieve.

However, if you've decided a live event is your way forward, the most effective way of ensuring it will return the best value it can is by following the proven steps in *The Facts Of Live* right from the tipping point and ensuring you and your team, or those you bring on board, adopt the principles we've detailed throughout the process.

The impact of a live event will be greatest when its purpose is clear and you have the right team in place at the right time with the relevant content and contextual experience, empowered and supported to make the decisions they need to make. This ensures that everyone's expertise, skills, craftsmanship and efforts are focused, by means of strong leadership, on what matters: the purpose and/or creative integrity of the live event.

Throughout *The Facts Of Live*, I have documented proven, pragmatic and practical foundations and principles you need to be able to capitalise on the powerful medium of live events. We've looked at the art and the science: the science of knowing how to set up your team most effectively and the processes you need to encourage to get the best out of those producing the art – the content – leaving your audience feeling moved to think differently, enjoy great entertainment, or buy more of your stuff.

Life is about experiences.
Find them or create them.

And Finally

Here are a final few thoughts and details about some additional resources to help you now and at any time in the future.

Whenever you need a quick reference guide to the key principles and foundations in *The Facts Of Live*, you can find guidance and tools at:

www.TheFactsOfLive.com

Over to you

A large part of my life consists of either planning or going on adventures and expeditions, or working in the live events sphere. Both these fields of activity offer similar rewards. The adventures and expeditions are, for me anyway, about embracing the natural world: a world constantly producing live spectacles and experiences more impressive, awe inspiring and moving than we humans could ever hope to produce artificially. These experiences always evoke a sense of wonder and curiosity in me.

Live events, produced and created well, can offer similar exhilaration. At the very least, they should make people stop and think. They're the most powerful medium that exists to manipulate the senses and evoke a whole range of emotions. It's why I love creating them.

I believe life is for filling with experiences – those you go and find, be it in nature or anywhere else, and those you create.

It's also another reason I wrote this book. The more people I can help create more exciting, engaging or powerful live events and experiences, the better. If I can make the experience more enjoyable and profitable for you, too, better still.

You're not alone as you do so. You have this book as initial guidance and foundations and there's an online resource to accompany it, for you to use anytime.

The Facts Of Live website

As I have mentioned, there is a reference guide to accompany this book at www.TheFactsOfLive.com. It's an easy-to-use, largely visual tool to help with:

- Content and context analysis
- The live cycle
- Team structures (with numerous examples)
- Tipping point options
- Procurement approaches and tools

There is also a Q & A section on the website. If you have any queries about the information and guidance in *The Facts Of Live*, you can submit them using the form on the website. From time to time, I will update the clarifications section with any amendments I feel relevant, based on the continuation of my own work and the requests I receive via the website, to provide you with information that is as current and relevant as it can be, and that continues to evolve to support as many people as possible. In other words, the clarifications section of www.TheFactsOfLive.com is a live version of *The Facts Of Live*.

If you would like recommendations on how to structure core teams for your event, you can submit a request on the site, too. Keep the event anonymous; you only need to provide enough information for me to understand the type of event and its component parts, along with your key queries. You will either be directed to an existing team structure on the site, or your team structure will be added to the website. Feel free to send any other queries, questions or requests to:

hello@TheFactsOfLive.com

I hope you have found *The Facts Of Live* both insightful and useful, and will continue to do so whenever you refer to it, or to the website, as your work with live events evolves.

Thanks for taking the time to read this book. I look forward to seeing you out there somewhere, creating ever more glorious and successful live events, armed with and empowered by *The Facts Of Live*.

Will Glendinning

www.TheFactsOfLive.com

Acknowledgements

Looking back on the last twenty years of my career, I'm amazed at what I've achieved, and it often feels a bit unreal. From my insane projects and Herculean challenges through to my constant striving to push boundaries and create ever more impactful events, I have been helped immeasurably by some key people. I'd like to take the opportunity to thank them here.

Thanks must go to Jack Raby for giving me my first break, my first proper job, with one of the most incredible companies in the world. I should probably say thanks to him for toughening me up, too.

It's hard to describe Gary Withers, founder of Imagination. I could write a whole book just on what I learned from him and his company. Gary, thanks for an apprenticeship like no other. Thanks, too, for your help and support after I left Imagination.

Thanks must also go to an incredible gentleman who is sadly no longer with us: Peter Price, or 'Pricey'. Pricey did two things. He taught me how to get the best out of people, and he stopped me from turning into an arrogant little so-and-so. Pricey, thank you.

A huge thank you to Ursula Morrish – for so much.

Thanks as well to Andrew Douglass for putting his faith in me, and for the opportunities that came with that faith.

Thank you to Robert Alge who, aside from being one of the most talented producers I've ever met or worked with, has always offered unwaveringly honest and insightful advice over the years.

I owe a huge thank you to Rachel Dulai and her long-suffering husband, Soma, for putting up with me and supporting me, way beyond the call of duty, as I built up my own business and ventures.

There are many other people I want to thank, too numerous to mention, from those who have hired and trusted me to those who have so willingly helped me over the years. These wonderful people include: Jo Aitken, Lucy Armstrong, Chenine Bhathena, Ian Braid, Kris Donaldson, Iain Edmondson, Efrosyni Konstantinou, Amanda Lumley, Tim Owen, James Shepheard-Walwyn, Geoff Summerton and Olivier Vallée.

Finally, thank you to my family: Lucy, Mum and Dad. If this book does nothing else, it may at least go some way towards explaining just what it is I've been doing since I left home!

The Author

Will Glendinning is an executive producer, director, designer and consultant. He is also an author and speaker, and regularly features in print, on TV and radio. He has worked for, run and built his own multimillion-pound companies and has had his work praised in Parliament.

Over the years, Will has been involved with and responsible for some of the most ambitious live events, exhibitions, pavilions, marketing campaigns and entertainment around the world in recent history. He's helped brands such as Coke, Samsung and UEFA, along with the Olympic and Paralympic Games and the Tour de France. He's worked with world leaders, and produced military ceremonies and cultural festivals, and he's supported the design and development of permanent live event spaces and venues. He's the expert the experts turn to.

Will loves a challenge and makes things happen, regardless of the obstacles. In the interests of producing and delivering live events that create the maximum impact for the best value possible, he has made overambitious creative ideas a reality, overcome political hurdles and restrictive budgets, battled Mother Nature and had to deal with terrorist threats.

When he's not dealing with live events, Will's challenges take on an even more adventurous form, from jumping out of helicopters with his snowboard to freediving in the coldest and most brutal places on earth. Be it adventures or events, though, Will enjoys finding or creating powerful experiences in the real world, live.

You can connect with Will and find out more about his work at:

Personal website:
www.WillGlendinning.com

The Facts Of Live website:
www.TheFactsOfLive.com

Printed in Great Britain
by Amazon